100% Student SUCCESS

AMY SOLOMON, MS, OTR

LORI TYLER, MS

TERRY TAYLOR, PhD

DELMAR
CENGAGE Learning

Australia • Brazil • Japan • Korea • Mexico • Singapore • Spain • United Kingdom • United States

DELMAR
CENGAGE Learning™

100% Student Success
Amy Solomon, MS, OTR, Lori Tyler, MS,
and Terry Taylor, PhD

Vice President, Career Education SBU:
Dawn Gerrain

Director of Learning Solutions:
Sherry Dickinson

Managing Editor: Robert L. Serenka, Jr.

Acquisitions Editor: Martine Edwards

Product Manager: Jennifer Anderson

Editorial Assistant: Falon Ferraro

Director of Production: Wendy A.
Troeger

Production Manager: J.P. Henkel

Content Project Manager: Amber Leith

Technology Project Manager:
Sandy Charette

Director of Marketing: Wendy E.
Mapstone

Channel Manager: Gerard McAvey

Marketing Coordinator:
Jonathan Sheehan

Cover and Text Design: Suzanne Nelson,
essence of 7

For product information and technology assistance, contact us
at **Cengage Learning Customer & Sales Support, 1-800-354-9706.**

For permission to use material from this text or product,
submit all requests online at **www.cengage.com/permissions.**
Further permissions questions can be emailed to
permissionrequest@cengage.com.

Library of Congress Control Number: 2006019209

ISBN-13: 978-1-4180-1630-2
ISBN-10: 1-4180-1630-6

Delmar
5 Maxwell Drive
Clifton Park, NY 12065
USA

Cengage Learning is a leading provider of customized learning solutions with
office locations around the globe, including Singapore, the United Kingdom,
Australia, Mexico, Brazil, and Japan. Locate your local office at:
www.cengage.com/global.

Cengage Learning products are represented in Canada by Nelson Education Ltd.

To learn more about Delmar, visit **www.cengage.com/delmar.**

Purchase any of our products at your local college store or at our preferred
online store **www.ichapters.com.**

NOTICE TO THE READER

Publisher does not warrant or guarantee any of the products described herein or perform any
independent analysis in connection with any of the product information contained herein.
Publisher does not assume, and expressly disclaims, any obligation to obtain and include
information other than that provided to it by the manufacturer.

The reader is expressly warned to consider and adopt all safety precautions that might be
indicated by the activities herein and to avoid all potential hazards. By following the instructions
contained herein, the reader willingly assumes all risks in connection with such instructions.

The Publisher makes no representation or warranties of any kind, including but not limited to,
the warranties of fitness for particular purpose or merchantability, nor are any such
representations implied with respect to the material set forth herein, and the publisher takes no
responsibility with respect to such material. The publisher shall not be liable for any special,
consequential, or exemplary damages resulting, in whole or part, from the readers' use of, or
reliance upon, this material.

The authors and Delmar Cengage Learning affirm that the Web site URLs referenced herein were
accurate at the time of printing. However, due to the fluid nature of the Internet, we cannot
guarantee their accuracy for the life of the edition.

Printed in Canada
6 7 8 9 11 10

Contents

3   LEARNING STRATEGIES 43

4   CRITICAL THINKING AND PROBLEM SOLVING 69

5 LEGAL AND ETHICAL ISSUES IN THE ACADEMIC ENVIRONMENT 89

6 NUTRITION AND FITNESS STRATEGIES FOR THE SUCCESSFUL STUDENT 109

9 COMMUNICATION SKILLS FOR STUDENT SUCCESS 179

10 HUMAN BEHAVIOR 199

Find It Fast

Need tips on taking effective notes in class?   See page 52

Want to create an effective study environment?   See page 54

Want to get more from your reading?   See pages 55–56

Need tips on solving math problems?   See page 57

Want to improve your test-taking abilities?   See pages 59–60

CRITICAL THINKING AND PROBLEM SOLVING 69

Need to assess your thinking process?   See page 73

Want to develop your critical thinking abilities?   See page 75

Looking for ways to think more creatively?   See page 79

LEGAL AND ETHICAL ISSUES
IN THE ACADEMIC ENVIRONMENT 89

Want to be informed about reporting cases of sexual harassment?
See page 94

Need suggestions for eliminating the need to cheat on exams?
See page 100

Want to know ways to avoid plagiarizing?   See page 101

Looking for effective conflict resolution techniques?   See page 103

NUTRITION AND FITNESS STRATEGIES
FOR THE SUCCESSFUL STUDENT 109

Want to make wiser food choices?   See page 116

Need to improve your sleep habits?   See page 119

Want to develop an exercise routine?   See page 120

Need to improve your posture?   See page 123

FINANCIAL CONSIDERATIONS
FOR SCHOOL SUCCESS. 131

Need to create a budget and spending plan?
See pages 134–135

Need tips on completing financial aid forms?
See page 139

Want tips on the process of renting?
See page 142

Need advice on purchasing a home?
See page 144

Want suggestions for purchasing a car?
See page 144

INFORMATION LITERACY FOR
THE TWENTY-FIRST CENTURY. 155

Want to know how to use a periodical index?
See page 167

Want to learn how to use Boolean operators to search
the World Wide Web? See page 169

Need guidance on the research process?
See page 172

COMMUNICATION SKILLS
FOR STUDENT SUCCESS. 179

Need to develop more effective listening skills?
See page 182

Looking for guidance in understanding
body language? See page 182

Preface

CONGRATULATIONS!

Welcome to the world of college! Your enrollment in college says that you have made a decision to grow and develop as a person and professional. Your college experience will provide valuable knowledge and insights over the course of your lifetime. *100% Student Success* will provide you with tools to develop your professional and personal skills and to accomplish your goals.

FORGET YOUR TECHNICAL SKILLS

Well, for a while anyway. Your technical skills are important, of course, and developing skills for a profession is likely to be the reason you enrolled in college. However, there are skills in addition to technical ones that will add to your success as a student and make you more desirable as an employee upon graduation. You may have heard of "soft skills," "generic skills," or "professional behaviors." Each of these terms refers to *self-management skills,* the ability to relate well to others, to work collaboratively, and to work ethically and with integrity. Your future employers will value these skills— sometimes over and beyond your technical expertise. Developing these skills in school will provide a strong foundation for entering the workplace upon your graduation.

HOW WILL THIS TEXT HELP YOU?

100% Student Success covers topics that are fundamental to professional success. The following are the main themes from the topics in the text. Take a look at these to get a general idea of the book and to see how each topic supports you in your academic success.

▶ **ELEMENTS OF SUCCESS IN COLLEGE:** You will learn general skills needed for success in college. The abilities to communicate, organize yourself, and interact effectively are examples of success skills. Understanding the importance of these general skills will prepare you for developing them further.

▶ **ADDRESSING DETERRENTS SUCCESSFULLY:** You will learn how to address common deterrents faced by college students that can adversely affect persistence in school. By taking proactive and positive steps, you can remain focused and achieve your goals.

▶ **FINDING OUT ABOUT LEARNING STYLES AND SKILLS:** Have you ever wondered how you learn best? What is your learning style? Do you understand the impact your learning style can have on your success in school? Knowing your learning style will help you choose the appropriate study activities from which you will learn best. You will explore your learning style and the activities that support it.

▶ **DEVELOPING CRITICAL AND CREATIVE THINKING SKILLS:** Sound reasoning and thinking give you credibility. You will explore steps for critical and creative thinking and apply them to everyday activities.

▶ **UNDERSTANDING THE LEGAL AND ETHICAL ISSUES THAT AFFECT YOU:** As a student, you have specific rights and responsibilities. You will learn about your role in addressing legal and ethical issues.

▶ **SELF-MANAGEMENT:** Personal management skills such as taking care of your health, managing your finances, and understanding your own behavior and others' behavior are important components of success. You will explore how these elements affect your learning and you will master techniques for managing them successfully.

HOW TO USE THIS BOOK

100% Student Success is written to actively involve you in developing positive and productive personal and professional skills. The following features will help guide you through the material and provide opportunities for you to practice what you've learned:

▶ **THE "BIG PICTURE:"** The Big Picture, provided at the beginning of each chapter, is a kind of site map intended to give you an overview of chapter contents in relation to the other chapters in the text. As you read through the material, you are encouraged to recognize and consider the relationships among the various concepts and pieces of information you are learning.

▶ **LEARNING OBJECTIVES:** Learning objectives outline the information in each chapter. Use them to identify the important points and to understand what you are supposed to learn. Also, use learning objectives as a tool to measure what you have mastered and what you still need to work on. You are encouraged to expand on these objectives according to your goals and interests.

▶ **TOPIC SCENARIOS:** At the beginning of each chapter, a scenario demonstrates the application of chapter concepts to the real world. Use the questions following each scenario to stimulate your critical thinking and analytical skills. Discuss the questions with classmates. You are encouraged to think of your own ideas regarding how to apply concepts and to raise additional questions.

▶ **REFLECTION QUESTIONS:** Reflection questions ask you to evaluate your personal development. This section is intended to increase your self-awareness and ability to understand your decisions and actions.

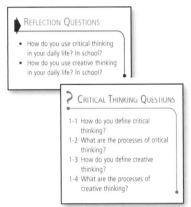

▶ REFLECTION QUESTIONS

- How do you use critical thinking in your daily life? In school?
- How do you use creative thinking in your daily life? In school?

❓ CRITICAL THINKING QUESTIONS

1-1 How do you define critical thinking?
1-2 What are the processes of critical thinking?
1-3 How do you define creative thinking?
1-4 What are the processes of creative thinking?

▶ **CRITICAL THINKING QUESTIONS:** Critical thinking questions challenge you to examine ideas and to thoughtfully apply concepts presented in the text. These questions encourage the development of thinking skills, which are crucial for efficient performance in school and in the workplace.

▶ **APPLY IT!:** After many sections of the text, you will find activities that help you apply to real-life situations the concepts discussed in the section. Your instructor may assign these as part of the course requirements. If they are not formally assigned, it will be helpful to complete them for your own development. There are three types of activities available:

- **Individual Activities** are directed at your personal development.
- **Group Activities** typically include projects that are more successfully completed with the addition of several perspectives or broad research. A team effort adds to the success of these learning projects.
- **Internet Activities** are intended to help you develop online skills. For example, you may research a topic or participate in an online discussion thread.

● **Find It Fast**

STRATEGIES FOR COLLEGE SUCCESS . . . .

Need tips on setting goals?   See pages 6–7

Want to know how to maintain your motivation level?
    See page 8

Looking for ways to stay organized?   See page 10

Need to improve your time management skills?   See page 11

LEARNING OBJECTIVES REVISITED

Review the learning objectives for this chapter and rate your level of achievement for each objective using the rating scale provided. For each objective
on which you do not rate yourself as a 3, outline a plan of action that you
will take to fully achieve the objective. Include a time frame for this plan.

1 = did not successfully achieve objective

2 = understand what is needed, but need more study or practice

3 = achieved learning objective thoroughly

	1	2	3
Explain the importance of goal setting.	☐	☐	☐
Explain how technology has affected the need for continued education.	☐	☐	☐
Discuss what it means to be a responsible student.	☐	☐	☐
Describe how effective communication can affect the classroom experience.	☐	☐	☐
Describe the impact that attitude and motivation can have on your academic experience.	☐	☐	☐
Demonstrate the ability to set goals and identify the steps to achieve the set goals.	☐	☐	☐
Explain and demonstrate an understanding of time management.	☐	☐	☐
Demonstrate the ability to create a budget.	☐	☐	☐

Steps to Achieve Unmet Objectives

Steps   Due Date

1. _____   _____

2. _____   _____

3. _____   _____

4. _____   _____

You may find it helpful to combine the activity types. For example, an individual project may require Internet research. Some individual activities can be adapted to group activities, and vice versa. Use the activities as guides and modify them in ways that best support your learning.

▶ **SUCCESS STEPS:** Success steps are included throughout the text and provide concise steps for achieving various goals. They are offered as a summary of each process. Details of each step are discussed fully in the body of the text. Are you looking for success steps to achieve a specific goal? Use the "Find It Fast" section in the front of the book to locate the steps you need.

▶ **LEARNING OBJECTIVES AND LEARNING OBJECTIVES REVISITED:** Chapter learning objectives, like those provided on course syllabi, outline what you should be learning from the chapter. The learning objectives should guide you to the main concepts of the chapter. Refer back to the learning objectives frequently and pay attention to how chapter material adds to your knowledge related to each objective.

Learning Objectives Revisited provides an opportunity for you to assess the effectiveness of your learning and to set goals to expand your knowledge in a given area. The Learning Objectives Revisited grid and instructions for its use are found at the end of each chapter. The example shown on the left is taken from Chapter 1 of the *100% Student Success* textbook.

▶ **SUGGESTED ITEMS FOR LEARNING PORTFOLIO:** A portfolio is a collection of the work that you have done. A *learning portfolio* is used to track your progress through school and a *professional portfolio* showcases your professional accomplishments. A developmental portfolio typically contains documents that illustrate your development over time. A professional portfolio contains finished projects and work that represents your best efforts and achievements. Throughout *100% Student Success* there are suggestions to include completed activities in your portfolio. If you are using the *100% Success Portfolio Workbook* that is available as part of the *100% Success* series, you will have guidelines for organizing your portfolio. If you are not using the *100% Success Portfolio Workbook,* select items for your portfolio and arrange them in a way that illustrates your professional development and showcases your best work.

SUPPLEMENTARY MATERIALS

In addition to the textbook, the following supplemental materials are available:

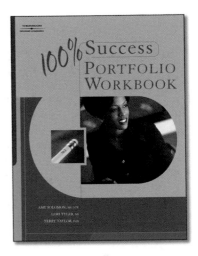

▶ **100% SUCCESS PORTFOLIO WORKBOOK:** This supplement to the text-book provides a format for creating your portfolio and expands on the applications of the concepts presented in the text. Elements of the portfolio guide include additional explanations of textbook content, guidelines for journaling, additional professional development resources, and references to online activities. The workbook is an optional component of the *100% Success* series. If you or your instructor has opted to use the workbook, follow the guidelines for completing the portfolio.

▶ **100% SUCCESS ONLINE COMPANION:** Textbook and portfolio activities are supported by additional resources located in the online companion. These resources include additional activities, assessments, and suggestions for expanding your development beyond what is included in the textbook. Access the online companion at http://www.delmarlearning.com/companions.

▶ **WEBTUTOR:** The WebTutor is an online course guide that complements *100% Student Success*. WebTutor provides you with tools to organize course content, track your progress in the course, and plan your projects. In addition to these organizational tools, the WebTutor provides links to helpful resources, access to discussion threads and support documents, such as study sheets and review quizzes.

BEYOND STUDENT SUCCESS

What are your goals for after you graduate? For most students, the typical goal is to become employed and achieve success in their field. Success begins with the skills you develop and practice in college. *100% Student Success* lays the foundation for the next two texts in the series of three books, *100% Job Search Success* and *100% Career Success*.

The professional skills such as self-management and communication that you practice and develop in school become skills that are desirable to employers. *100% Job Search Success* expands on the skills that you have practiced by applying them to finding the job of your choice. The third book in the series, *100% Career Success*, takes you into the workplace and provides strategies for using your skills to add to your success as an employee.

A FINAL WORD

Look ahead. As you read and complete the activities of *100% Student Success,* keep your long-term goals in mind. Keep professionalism foremost in your mind and think about how you can apply these concepts to your everyday activities. Application is the key—and the more you practice, the more successful you will be in school and as you enter the professional world.

Again, congratulations on your decision to attend college. May you have 100% success now and in the future.

Acknowledgments

The authors of the *100% Success Series* would like to thank the staff at Delmar Cengage Learning for their tireless support and editorial suggestions. Much appreciation also goes to our students, who have taught us so much over the years. Without them, this book would not have been possible.

We wish to recognize the educators and students who reviewed various components of *100% Student Success* throughout its development and contributed many thoughtful suggestions for the program.

Angela Alexander, Ph.D.
Nicholls State University
Thibodaux, Louisiana

Douglas Allen
Catawba Valley Community
    College
Hickory, North Carolina

Kim R. Barnett-Johnson
Ivy Tech Community College
Fort Wayne, Indiana

Ashley King Brown
Catawba Valley Community
    College
Hickory, North Carolina

Katheleene L. Bryan
Daytona Beach Community
    College
Daytona Beach, Florida

Bettye A. Easley
Grant College, Suffolk
    Community College
Brentwood, New York

Marianne Fitzpatrick
Oregon Coast Community
    College
Newport, Oregon

W. T. Hatcher
Aiken Technical College
Aiken, South Carolina

Irene Gordon Jasmine
Nicholls State University
Thibodaux, Louisiana

Aleyenne S. Johnson-Jonas, M.A.
Brown Mackie College
San Diego, California

Debra M. Klein
Suffolk County Community
    College
Selden, New York

Sara L. Morgan
Minnesota School of
    Business–Plymouth
Minneapolis, Minnesota

Kevin Pugh, M.S.Ed.
University of Colorado
    at Boulder
Boulder, Colorado

Susan R. Royce, M.S.
Design Institute of San Diego
San Diego, California

Leo Sevigny
Lyndon State College
Lyndonville, Vermont

Avette D. Ware
Suffolk County Community
    College
Selden, New York

©Anderson Ross/Getty Images

CHAPTER OUTLINE

1 Strategies for College Success

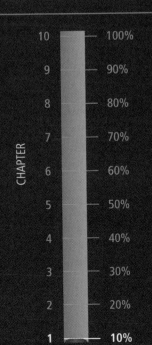

THE BIG PICTURE

LEARNING OBJECTIVES

By the end of this chapter, you will achieve the following objectives:

▶ Explain the importance of goal setting.

▶ Explain how technology has affected the need for continuing education.

▶ Discuss what it means to be a responsible student.

▶ Describe how effective communication can affect the classroom experience.

▶ Describe the impact that attitude and motivation can have on your academic experience.

▶ Demonstrate the ability to set goals and identify the steps to achieve those goals.

▶ Explain and demonstrate an understanding of time management.

▶ Explain the importance of maintaining a budget.

1

TOPIC SCENARIO

Drew Parsons had always seemed to struggle in school. Grades were never easy. However, Drew was determined to go to college. As an adult, prior to entering college, Drew decided it was time to figure out why school had always been difficult for him. He concluded that he was not going to repeat the same pattern of poor grades that had plagued him so far in his education experience. In trying to understand why he had struggled in school, Drew decided to evaluate certain areas in his life. These areas included his abilities in organization, time management, communication, taking responsibility, financial planning, and goal setting. Through self-reflection and honest evaluation, Drew discovered areas that in the past had affected his ability to do better academically.

After reaching some conclusions, Drew began to write down solutions that could help in his development of these lacking abilities. For instance, Drew was able to admit that due to his lack of organizational skills, he would sometimes forget assignments. He then set a goal to take good notes related to the assignments he would be given in his college studies. Drew also concluded that in the past rather than take responsibilities for his own failings, he had chosen to blame others. For his college studies, Drew decided that he would take responsibility for his own successes and failures. He also concluded that he would take the time needed to learn from those failures and grow, so that the pattern would not be repeated. Drew's desire to value his college education experience led him to become more self-aware. Drew's focus on his growth and development as an individual paid off. As a result of his efforts, Drew graduated from college and continues to experience great success in his profession.

Based on this short description of Drew's experience, answer the following questions:

- What is your responsibility for being a successful college graduate?

- What areas might you need to develop in order to become a better student?

- If you know of areas that may be stumbling blocks in your education experience, how will you overcome these areas in order to be successful in school?

STRATEGIES FOR COLLEGE SUCCESS: AN OVERVIEW

For some individuals, beginning a college course can be a daunting ordeal; for others, it is an immediately exciting adventure. Regardless of one's feelings related to starting school, all individuals typically have a strong desire for success. Arriving at success can be more challenging for some than for others. Most (if not all) individuals encounter roadblocks in their lives that can divert them from their goals. This textbook offers you information to help you take the responsibility to make your college experience an enjoyable journey, as well as to maximize your opportunities for successful program completion.

Chapter 1 provides a general overview of elements that are important to college success. It is intended to supply a big picture of the many considerations important to you as a college student. Subsequent chapters will provide more detailed strategies and information about these areas.

Setting goals and establishing sound habits now will contribute to your success as a student.

THE IMPORTANCE OF EDUCATION

Technology continues to advance, forcing society to develop methods that allow adaptation to change. One of the biggest changes that has affected society over the last few years is the increasing use of computers and the Internet. With these changes, society has had to adapt and learn. It is almost impossible not to be affected by the Internet. For example, the Internet has changed how education is offered, banking is accomplished, research is conducted, and advertising is achieved.

As these industries are affected by change, so are employees. New jobs are created and old job descriptions are revised to meet new demands and incorporate new technologies. Individuals who are willing and able to learn new technologies are most likely to be successful.

A degree in higher education offers many benefits. Not only does higher education enable people to gain skills and grow intellectually, education challenges individuals to broaden their understanding of the world around them. Employers continue to seek individuals who embrace changing technologies and who demonstrate an appreciation of ethnic and cultural diversity, competency in effective communication, and the ability to set goals and achieve them. Completing a college education is a unique opportunity to learn the technical skills needed to acquire a job and to learn and grow in areas that will benefit both future employers and your personal growth.

1

TAKING RESPONSIBILITY
FOR YOUR EDUCATION

Embracing your academic experience requires taking responsibility for what you learn. Taking responsibility begins with self-reflection and assessment of your goals, attitudes, and motivation.

GOAL SETTING

Goal setting is an important part of succeeding in college. By setting goals, you accomplish the following:

- ❱ You set a "road map" for where you want to go.
- ❱ You are able to select the most appropriate method(s) for reaching your goal.
- ❱ You are able to more easily gauge your progress toward your goal.
- ❱ You are able to make adjustments to your goal and methods as needed.
- ❱ You know when you have reached your goal and can appreciate your accomplishment.

success steps

The following success steps are based on suggestions made by Donohue (n.d.) for effective goal setting and achievement.

Step 1:   Set goals based on something that is important to you and something that you desire. Avoid letting someone else determine what your goals should be.

Step 2:   Make sure that your goals are complementary and do not conflict with one another.

Step 3:   In addition to professional areas, set goals that support spiritual, emotional, physical, and social needs.

Step 4:   State goals positively. For example, "I will study every night for two hours before doing other tasks" is more positive than "I won't do other tasks in the evening before studying."

Step 5:   Be as detailed and specific as possible when writing your goals. Goals should tell you what you will achieve, describe the conditions under which you will achieve the goal, and provide a time frame during which the goal will be achieved. In addition, goals should be measurable so that you meet a standard. For example, "I will study [what will be achieved] for two hours [measurable element] every weekday night [another measurable element] with no interruptions [conditions] throughout the fall semester [time frame]."

Step 6: Set your goals high enough to be challenging, but make them reasonable enough to be achievable.

Step 7: State your goals in writing. Written goals serve as a reminder and motivator and provide a guide to your success. Telling others about your goals may also contribute to goal achievement.

Breaking long-term goals into shorter-term goals allows you to see progress toward the longer-term goal. For example, completing a course successfully might be your long-term goal. By plotting out a schedule for completion of assignments over the term, each assignment becomes a short-term goal. Completion of each assignment brings you closer to achieving your long-term goal. Your progress is more obvious and rewarding when you recognize the accomplishment of smaller steps.

Another important aspect of goal setting is its cyclic nature. Achieving goals or steps toward them usually makes you aware of new areas for growth and learning, setting the stage for new goals. When you review your progress toward a goal, determine new goals that you can set for continued growth and development. Goal setting is an ongoing process that should continue as part of your lifelong learning.

When setting goals, make sure your goals represent short-term and long-term educational and professional plans. Once you have set your goals, strive to achieve each one. Upon successful completion of a goal, remember to recognize and reward your accomplishments in addition to being aware of opportunities for setting new goals.

Consider the diagram in Figure 1–1, which represents the process of goal setting and its relationship to your professional growth.

ATTITUDE AND MOTIVATION

Your attitude toward succeeding can directly impact your academic and overall life experiences. As in many other areas of life, school will have its ups and downs and there are times when you will encounter difficulties. Do not let problems become a roadblock to your success. Individuals who are able to use difficulties as opportunities to learn and develop solutions

? CRITICAL THINKING QUESTIONS

Stop here to consider the following questions. Take time to respond in writing and then reflect on your answers.

1–1. What are your long-term and short-term goals? What are you trying to accomplish?

1–2. Why is school important to your goals?

▶ REFLECTION QUESTION

- What is your attitude toward learning?

▶ REFLECTION QUESTIONS

- What motivates you to learn?
- Reflect on your motivation to do well in class. What do you really want from your education?
- How can you use your motivators help you to reach your education goals?

1

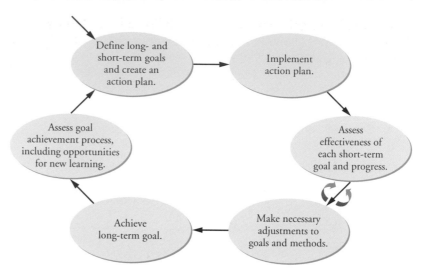

FIGURE 1-1.   The Goal-setting cycle. Goal setting is a series of sequential steps that involve setting a plan of action, assessing the steps to take, and setting new goals based on what you learn and the interests that develop during goal achievement. You are likely to repeat the process of assessing and adjusting short-term goals, indicated by the solid blue arrows.

will be valued in the classroom and later as professionals. Barriers commonly faced by adult learners and methods of addressing them are covered in Chapter 2.

Learning to remain motivated during difficult situations is a valuable lesson that will make a difference to your success in school, in your career, and in other life circumstances.

! RESOURCE BOX

RESOURCES TO HELP WITH MAINTAINING MOTIVATION
- Study groups
- Tutors
- Instructors
- Campus resource centers
- Academic advisor

REFLECTION QUESTION

- What other methods might you personally find helpful for addressing difficulties in school?

success steps

Consider the following steps for maintaining your motivation:

1. Clearly identify your motivators.

2. Ensure that your motivators are realistic. For example, if you identify a reward for yourself, make sure it is something you can realistically do or afford.

3. Keep your motivators "top of mind" so that they remain visible and you are aware of them.

Motivation can be a significant factor in the ability to learn. Motivated individuals tend to solve problems and seek out methods that will help them overcome and achieve in difficult areas.

GETTING THE MOST OUT OF EVERY CLASS

Getting the most from every class has specific benefits, including acquiring the most education for your investment of time and money, preparing to the best of your ability for your future career, and achieving self-improvement. Fully participating in and being actively involved in your classes allows you to gain a better perspective on and appreciation for others' beliefs and ideals. The diversity of today's workforce requires that you develop an understanding and acceptance of a wide range of cultures, beliefs, lifestyles, and other unique aspects of individuals.

In the scenario presented at the beginning of this chapter, Drew Parsons had the desire to make the most of his education. His quest to accomplish this included evaluating and developing skills in areas such as organization, time management, communication, and financial planning. Drew concluded that not having these skills could adversely affect his level of success in school and in his career.

ORGANIZATION

Becoming organized can be quite challenging for some individuals. The concept of being organized can vary considerably between individuals. Organization includes the components of time and materials management as well as the ability to manage tasks and information efficiently. The rest of Chapter 1 and the remaining chapters in *100% Student Success* address these elements in greater detail. For now, consider how these components contribute to your organizational skills and which elements might be important for you to improve.

The first step toward improving organizational abilities is understanding your need to improve and determining where improvement is needed. Organization can impact function at home, in school, and at work. In addition, organization is a key factor in learning. The brain processes well-organized information more effectively than information that is presented in random order. Your ability to organize information will directly affect your mastery of course information. To get the most out of each of your classes, try implementing the following organizational steps.

©Digital Vision

Positive expectations and active participation will help you to gain the most benefits from your classes.

▶ REFLECTION QUESTIONS

- What are your expectations regarding your classes?
- What do you want and hope to get out of each of your classes?
- What specific things can you do to make sure you get the most out of every class?

▶ REFLECTION QUESTIONS

- How effective are your organizational skills?
- How can you improve your organizational skills?
- What organizational strategies work well for you? How can they be applied to organizing for school?

success steps

DEVELOPING ORGANIZATIONAL SKILLS

Step 1: Assess your current organizational skills and then develop an action plan to improve where needed.

Step 2: Use the Internet as a resource to develop your organizational skills. Conduct a search using "organizational skills" and "organizational methods" and select resources that are relevant to your needs.

Step 3: Begin to work on organizing your classroom activities. Work toward organizing your notes, tests, activities, study area, times for studying and completing homework, and so forth. Select filing and archiving systems that work for you.

Step 4: Develop charts, diagrams, flow charts, tables, lists, and other tools that can help in organizing the information you are trying to learn.

Step 5: Don't procrastinate. Disorganization sometimes stems from not following through in a timely manner, as tasks and materials tend to pile up. Take the necessary time to complete assignments and projects thoroughly and well. Procrastination results in the need to rush, and rushing can create disorganized work.

Step 6: Complete assignments on or ahead of an established schedule so that you have time to think them through in a well-organized fashion as well as review them.

TIME MANAGEMENT

Many students have very full lives. In addition to school, time is often split between work and taking care of parents, children, spouses, and the home. In addition, extracurricular activities that support personal and professional interests must often be factored into the schedule. Finding time to accomplish all the tasks related to each of these responsibilities can be overwhelming. Accomplishing all of these tasks successfully requires effective time management skills.

Good time management starts with assessing what must typically be accomplished for each day and the time available to complete each task. According to Blush (2005), effective time management includes the following success steps:

success steps

TIME MANAGEMENT SKILLS

Step 1: Focus on one thing at a time. Multitasking can dilute your attention and may not be as efficient as concentrating on one task at a time. Complex tasks require concentrated attention.

Step 2: Prioritize your tasks. There will be times when all tasks simply cannot be completed in the amount of time that you have available. In those cases, prioritizing and completing the most pressing tasks first is necessary.

Step 3: Assess the amount of time each task requires. Schedule the task when you have the appropriate amount of time for it, and reserve the time for that task. Determine the tasks and task components that are essential and eliminate nonessential elements.

Step 4: Don't procrastinate unenjoyable tasks. Get them done in a timely manner and reward yourself for the accomplishment. One suggestion is to complete less enjoyable tasks first to get them out of the way. Your motivation to complete them is getting to the more enjoyable tasks.

Step 5: Make a realistic daily schedule and to-do list based on the amount of time needed for each task. Print out the list each day and refer to it as needed to stay focused on what must be completed. Periodically check your progress and adjust the schedule as needed. Identify specific times for phone calls, meetings, and other duties. If a task is not completed, move it to your list for the following day.

Step 6: Establish a weekly game plan. Determine projects and goals on a weekly basis and then break them down into daily tasks.

Step 7: Determine your most productive time of day. Use that time to complete the most important tasks. Routine tasks should be accomplished during lower-energy periods.

Time management practices and time concepts vary considerably across cultures. You may have time concepts and management methods that reflect your culture or how you were raised. Likewise, other individuals that you encounter in school and in the workplace may also have their unique perspectives. To function effectively in school and in the workplace, it is important to understand these differences and how they interface with school

1

and workplace demands. If you recognize time management practices in a colleague that seem to contradict Western expectations, consider that the differences might be cultural. Consider how to address scheduling and time-related issues with tact and respect.

There are a variety of tools available for time and life management. These tools include both paper and electronic planning systems. Examples of paper planning systems include daily, weekly, and monthly calendars in a variety of bound and desk calendar formats. Electronic solutions include personal digital assistants (PDAs) and software programs that are compatible with various computer operating systems. All time management tools accomplish the same task. The one that you choose will depend on your preference for paper or electronic formats.

? CRITICAL THINKING QUESTIONS

1–3. To test your ability in time management, consider the following scenario and answer the question.

Jan has just started college and is struggling to manage all the areas in her life that need attention. Jan is a single mom with two preschool kids. She has a full-time job and is taking classes four nights a week at the local college. Jan is having difficulty finding time to study. After reviewing the following schedule, how would you help Jan find more time to study?

6:00 a.m.—Kids up
7:00 a.m.—Leave for day care
7:30 a.m.—Drop kids off at day care
8:00 a.m.–4:00 p.m.—Work
4:30 p.m.—Pick kids up from day care; drop off at home with evening sitter
5:30 p.m.–9:30 p.m.—Evening classes (Monday and Wednesday)
6:00 p.m.–8:30 p.m.—Evening classes (Tuesday and Thursday)
10:00 p.m.–10:30 p.m.—Do household chores
10:30 p.m.–11:30 p.m.—Study
11:30 p.m.—In bed

apply it

Web Research

GOAL: *To research time management tools offered online.*

STEP 1: Conduct an Internet search using "electronic time management tools" as your search term. Explore the types of tools that are available.

STEP 2: Explore the time management tools that you find as a result of your search. Assess and compare the benefits and shortcomings of each based on your personal needs and preferences. Make a decision regarding which would best support your time management efforts.

STEP 3: Write a brief report on your evaluation. Explain and give reasons for your choice of tools. Be prepared to share this information with your classmates.

STEP 4: Consider placing this evaluation in your Learning Portfolio.

apply it

Analysis of Paper Planning Systems

GOAL: *To analyze types of paper planning systems.*

STEP 1: As a group, compile a list of paper planning systems.

STEP 2: Assign a planning system to each group member so duplication does not occur. Visit an office superstore or other office supplier and review the various paper planning systems.

1

Review your assigned paper planning system and record relevant information about it, including price, binding systems, features, and other information.

STEP 3: Bring your information back to the group and conduct a comparison of the various types of paper systems available. Discuss the advantages and disadvantages of each system.

STEP 4: Write a brief analysis of each system and your comparison and share your report with the class.

COMMUNICATION

Communicating effectively is a requirement of most professions. The classroom and academic activities provide an excellent venue for developing and practicing communication skills. Effective communication is another factor in getting the most from each course and learning effectively. Effective communication enhances your performance in a variety of classroom activities, including the following:

▶ **Group activities and discussions.** Students working in groups depend on each other for clear communication. The success of group activities requires that participants follow through on required tasks and communicate their progress and concerns with other group members. Group discussion is successful when all participants are willing to share their views as well as respect the views of others. Active participation in group discussion contributes to the learning process and typically increases the relevance and interest of the activity by providing a variety of perspectives and ideas.

▶ **Reflection and critical thinking questions.** Employers seek individuals who have skills in problem solving and critical thinking. Students who develop these skills and are able to effectively and logically communicate their thought processes are likely to be desirable employees.

▶ **Instructor and student interactions.** The ability to communicate questions and concerns to the instructor in an effective manner adds to your ability to benefit from course material. Appropriately addressing issues regarding your learning experience is critical to your satisfaction with school and will contribute to your ability to assertively address issues in the workplace.

1

▶ **Individual presentations.** Assignments requiring group and individual presentations provide the opportunity to develop skills in communicating with an audience. Giving thoughtful, organized presentations and participating as an active listener to other students' presentations adds to effective communication skills.

Communication is another area that can be significantly influenced by cross-cultural diversity. Western culture values assertiveness, asking questions, and stating individual ideas and opinions. Individuals who have been raised with other communication values and practices may not respond comfortably to expectations in Western classrooms or work situations. For example, individuals from certain cultures may find it disrespectful to disagree with the instructor or supervisor, who is viewed as an authority figure. It is important to be aware of and sensitive to diverse communication practices. There are situations in which individuals may need coaching in developing the skills that will support their success in the Western work environment.

Getting the most out of your college courses also requires you to utilize the communication tools that are available to inform you about class and institutional requirements. Understanding these elements will help you understand expectations, know deadlines, and prepare effectively for class. Consider the following tools, which play a significant role in the classroom communication and with which you are probably familiar:

▶ **The syllabus.** The syllabus communicates what you should expect to learn and the grading requirements of the class. Clearly stated objectives should be used as a guide for what will be accomplished in the course. It is up to you to communicate to the instructor if you are unclear about any parts of the syllabus or if you are not achieving course objectives.

▶ **Grades.** Grades communicate whether you are accomplishing the required tasks and achieving an understanding of the material. If your grades are below expectations, it is important for you and the instructor to agree on a course of action in as timely a manner as possible. It is your responsibility to approach the instructor if you have concerns. If you disagree with an instructor regarding a grade, clear and assertive (rather than aggressive) communication and negotiation skills become important. Briefly, assertive communication means that you state your point in a conversational tone, express your perspective and feelings versus blaming the other person, and demonstrate respect for the other point of view. Approaching the situation with an open mind and in a spirit of negotiation is also helpful. Assertive communication often results

1

in increased respect between student and instructor and a clearer understanding of expectations for future assignments.

▶ **Classroom and school policies and procedures.** Written policies and procedures communicate to students the expectations of instructors and school officials. You must review these policies and procedures and clarify what is unclear, as you are responsible for the content of the policies and procedures that affect you. Written communication in the form of deadlines, policies, and postings from school administration and instructors provides information that is critical to your success. For example, published deadlines for dropping courses without adverse consequences are important in the event that you need to drop a course. Pay attention to institutional and classroom bulletins and notices.

FINANCIAL CONSIDERATIONS

Sharon Ferrett (1997, p. 414) points out that "like time, money is a resource to manage and invest. As with time management, a financial planning system should not be rigid or constricting—it should give you freedom and flexibility." Properly managed finances can provide greater financial freedom than haphazardly managed resources. Ferrett lists the following elements of financial management:

▶ **Long-range financial planning.** Analyze short- and long-term financial goals.

▶ **A budget.** Establish a realistic budget and monitor it on a weekly basis to ensure that expenses and funds remain within your limits.

▶ **A good credit rating.** A good credit rating significantly affects the achievement of future financial goals.

▶ **Unexpected events.** Having a reserve for unexpected events is important to staying on track with financial goals. If unexpected events are not anticipated, financial goals can be negatively affected, with long-term consequences.

Lack of financial planning can negatively affect your schooling as well as your future. Establishing a well-thought-out budget will help to alleviate the stress that can come with bills. A budget provides a clear picture of income and outflow of money and will require you to analyze how you spend. Although this process at times may be challenging, budgeting and financial planning will lead to sound future financial practices.

An employer may request an applicant's credit scores prior to hiring. A high credit score can indicate that the individual has been financially responsible and stable. Good credit is established by paying bills on time and

? CRITICAL THINKING QUESTIONS

1–4. Why is keeping a budget critical to success in college and as you enter the workforce?

1–5. How can financial planning affect your future career goals, negatively and positively?

1

avoiding excessive debt. Credit reports are available from the three nation-wide credit bureaus: Equifax, Experian, and TransUnion.

Credit card debt can be a significant issue for those who have never managed their money. Most credit card companies charge a high interest rate, which often means individuals struggle just to make the minimum payment. In this situation, getting ahead financially becomes difficult. If high credit card bills become an issue, consider taking the following steps:

▶ Stop using credit cards.

▶ If you must have a credit card, use only one or two.

▶ Use credit only in emergency situations. If you do use a credit card, make sure you can pay the bill off at the end of the month.

▶ Never pay just the minimum amount. If possible, pay double or triple the minimum amount to get the balance paid off as quickly as possible.

▶ Consolidate your bills to a lower interest rate and then begin to pay off the consolidated amount. Once this is accomplished, beware of old habits. Don't repeat the same behavior.

▶ Call the credit card company and find out if a better interest rate is possible.

▶ Pay off one card, then add the amount you were paying on that card to the second. When the second is paid, contribute the sum of those two payments to the third, and so forth. Continue in this manner until all balances are paid.

Chapter 7 discusses financial management in greater detail.

CHAPTER SUMMARY

This chapter introduced you to the changing workplace and the new demands that rapid advancements make on individuals in the workplace. This chapter emphasized goal setting as well as foundational elements such as personal organization and time management, money management, and maximizing the benefit you derive from your education. These basic self-management tools will lay the foundation for developing and refining your skills using the information and activities in the remainder of *100% Student Success*.

Throughout this textbook, consider how what you learn supports you in developing basic self-management skills. More detailed information in these areas will help you to select from and personalize a variety of methods that will support your development as a student and provide the basis for becoming a successful professional.

POINTS TO KEEP IN MIND

In this chapter, numerous main points were discussed.

▌ Advances in technology continue to have an impact on the need for new jobs and individual skill requirements.

▌ Higher education offers the opportunity to gain skills and grow intellectually, in addition to broadening your view of the world.

▌ Taking responsibility for your education experience begins with self-reflection and assessment of your goals, attitudes, and motivation.

▌ Setting goals should incorporate both short-term steps and long-term plans.

▌ Written goals that are specific and measurable are more likely to be accomplished than unwritten and unspecific goals.

▌ Individuals who see opportunity in and learn from difficulties will be valued in the classroom and later as professionals.

▌ Persevering and completing difficult tasks will pay off.

▌ Understanding your need to improve and identifying specific areas for improvement are the first steps in developing your organizational abilities.

▌ Time management requires focusing on what needs to be accomplished and determining the amount of time available for each task.

▌ Time management tools include both paper and electronic planning systems.

▌ Communication tools for the classroom include the syllabus, grades, and classroom and school policies and procedures.

▌ Establishing a realistic budget and monitoring that budget on a weekly basis is critical for financial planning success.

▌ Good credit scores may be a requirement for employment.

LEARNING OBJECTIVES REVISITED

Review the learning objectives for this chapter and rate your level of achievement for each objective using the rating scale provided. For each objective on which you do not rate yourself as a 3, outline a plan of action that you will take to fully achieve the objective. Include a time frame for this plan.

1 = did not successfully achieve objective

2 = understand what is needed, but need more study or practice

3 = achieved learning objective thoroughly

1

	1	2	3
Explain the importance of goal setting.	☐	☐	☐
Explain how technology has affected the need for continued education.	☐	☐	☐
Discuss what it means to be a responsible student.	☐	☐	☐
Describe how effective communication can affect the classroom experience.	☐	☐	☐
Describe the impact that attitude and motivation can have on your academic experience.	☐	☐	☐
Demonstrate the ability to set goals and identify the steps to achieve the set goals.	☐	☐	☐
Explain and demonstrate an understanding of time management.	☐	☐	☐
Demonstrate the ability to create a budget.	☐	☐	☐

Steps to Achieve Unmet Objectives

Steps   Due Date

1. _____   _____

2. _____   _____

3. _____   _____

4. _____   _____

SUGGESTED ITEMS FOR LEARNING PORTFOLIO

▶ Analysis of Paper Planning Systems
▶ Web Research

REFERENCES

Blush, C. (2005). Time-management skills are crucial. The Arizona Republic Online Print Edition. Retrieved February 7, 2005, from http://www.azcentral.com/arizonarepublic/careerbuilder/articles/0116jobsmain16.html

Donohue, G. (n.d.). Goal setting: Powerful written goals in 7 easy steps! Retrieved February 1, 2005, from http://www.topachievement.com/goalsetting.html

Ferrett, S. K. (1997). *Peak Performance: Success in College and Beyond* (2nd ed.). Westerville, OH: McGraw-Hill.

1

CHAPTER OUTLINE

2

Common Concerns of the Adult College Student

THE BIG PICTURE

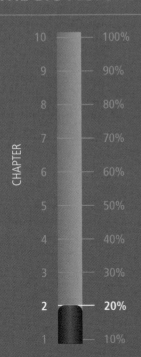

LEARNING OBJECTIVES

By the end of this chapter, you will achieve the following objectives:

▶ Define issues, barriers, and deterrents common to students in various situations.

▶ Identify methods of addressing barriers and deterrents and locate resources for addressing them.

▶ Describe professionalism and professional conduct and demonstrate it through actions and behavior.

▶ Devise a professional development plan for transition to the workplace.

2

TOPIC SCENARIO

Lindsay Dillon is a single parent who works as a receptionist for a physician at a family practice. She recently enrolled in an evening Medical Assisting Program at a local technical college, which she attends after her daytime job. She has two children, both in elementary school. Lindsay's mother lives in the same town and works three days a week. She is willing to help with child care on her days off but is unable to offer assistance on the days that she does work. Lindsay is the first in her peer group to attend college. In addition, she hasn't been in school for 15 years, when she attempted a nursing program but dropped out to have her family. Lindsay wonders how she is going to balance caring for her children, being employed full time, and keeping her friends while still succeeding in school. Based on Lindsay's situation, answer the following questions:

- Think about your personal situation and your academic training. How do Lindsay's challenges relate to those that you face?
- How can Lindsay find a way to balance all of her responsibilities? What are some resources that might be available to her?
- What challenges do you think Lindsay might face from her friends?
- What feelings might Lindsay have regarding returning to school after 15 years?

"ADULT" AND "TRADITIONAL AGE" STUDENTS

Adult college students can be defined as those over the age of 25 who have life experience outside the classroom (Imel, 2001). Traditional age students are those who are younger and have had minimal life experience. An example of the adult student might be the 40-year-old mother of two with a nursing background who is returning to school for an additional degree. An example of a traditional student is the new high school graduate, entering college for the first time. Today it is not unusual to have a blend of both types of students in the classroom.

There are certainly variations on these definitions. There are older students who have never been to college and there are younger students with considerable experience and insight. Use the information in this chapter to identify your needs and resources, regardless of how you fit the definitions of adult and traditional student.

School responsibilities are just one commitment of the adult student. Thoughtful planning and organization can contribute to effectively meeting the challenges of multiple tasks.

THE GREAT BALANCING ACT

It is generally recognized that adult students have multiple responsibilities, including family, financial obligations, employment commitments, and the daily concerns of home management. When school is added into this complex picture, the situation becomes even more challenging for the adult learner. The learner who enters the college environment with these priorities may have different concerns from the student who does not have the same responsibilities.

Students commonly have at least one of these responsibilities. For example, many college students who are considered traditional age have employment commitments and/or families. Students who do not have these types of responsibilities may face other issues, such as adjusting to the college environment, which requires management of time, priorities, and finances. Although adult students are typically viewed as having more commitments than others, all college students have responsibilities that require awareness of self and resources.

Regardless of whether you are a traditional or adult student, the great balancing act is successfully achieved by making sure that all priorities are effectively met—and this is sometimes easier said than done. Meeting priorities effectively means making careful assessments, knowing your resources, and engaging in creative problem solving. Often, balancing outside responsibilities and school will require making choices based on your priorities at a given time. It also means communicating with instructors and taking responsibility for your decisions.

PRIORITIES IN LIFE

If you have children, you know how illness can interfere with the daily routine. If you don't have children of your own, consider parents, friends, or colleagues who do have children. An ill child presents a significant challenge when the caregiver must be at work or school. Caring for elderly family members or attending to household emergencies can also require immediate attention.

School, gainful employment, family, and home are all *priorities* in your life. At times certain priorities (such as an ill family member) become more *pressing*. In other words, the more pressing priority requires your focus at a given time and is the priority that receives your immediate attention. Temporarily giving your attention to a more pressing issue does not mean that other aspects of your life are less of a priority—they still are—but they are not the topic of current focus.

SETTING PRIORITIES RESPONSIBLY

Most instructors are accepting of the fact that students are juggling a variety of commitments; they recognize that life sometimes makes demands other than those related to school. The student's responsibility is to prioritize coursework along with other life responsibilities. Although most students set priorities respectfully and appropriately, some do not. Problems arise when students make excuses and when other aspects of life continually take priority over school assignments. It is important to recognize that instructors must comply with certain regulations and that this puts constraints on how flexible they can be with students. For example, schools often have attendance requirements to meet regulations associated with receiving federal funding for various programs. Instructors are obligated to uphold these requirements. Students who consistently neglect school responsibilities put instructors in a precarious situation, which sometimes results in policies that are restrictive and seem disrespectful of students' other commitments. It is important to set your priorities responsibly and to communicate your reasons and intentions to your instructor. Keep in mind the important concept of setting priorities responsibly as you read the remaining sections of Chapter 2.

success steps

SETTING PRIORITIES

Step 1: Know your priorities and understand how to determine when some are more pressing than others.

Step 2: Make thoughtful decisions regarding prioritizing and communicate professionally with instructors about your needs.

Step 3: Understand the deterrents that adult learners commonly face during their education.

Step 4: Understand your responses to deterrents and select a constructive response from your resources.

Step 5: Develop professional behaviors and a professional presentation style.

HELPFUL AND RESPONSIBLE ATTITUDES

An attitude that reflects an understanding of the instructor's position, balanced with an assertive approach, contributes to effectively balancing priorities. The following suggestions are provided for you to consider as methods for maintaining a positive and helpful attitude.

▶ **Keep your long-term goal in mind.** Your ultimate goal is to achieve your educational objective by graduating and entering the profession that you have chosen to pursue. Remember that the stresses of being a student and carrying out your other life responsibilities are temporary. Remind yourself of the rewards that await you. Each challenge that you overcome is a step toward meeting your long-term goal.

▶ **Negotiate and compromise.** Instructors typically respond positively to being approached in a nondemanding manner that reflects a desire to honor school as well as other life commitments. Present your case, let the instructor know you are trying to manage your "balancing act," understand the instructor's commitments and responsibilities, and seek a middle ground that respects both of you. Use compromise to negotiate a workable solution.

▶ **Imagine you're in the workplace.** If you faced the same dilemma in the workplace, you would need to address the situation with your supervisor and devise a mutually workable solution to your dilemma. Interact in a manner that would be appropriate in the workplace and incorporate elements of professionalism, tact, and assertiveness in your communication with your instructor.

▶ **Weigh your options.** If you believe that you truly have a dilemma that cannot be resolved by negotiation and compromise, you may need to consider other alternatives. You may elect to choose your most pressing priority and accept consequences for doing so. You may seek outside support from the appropriate resource at your school. The ultimate decision is up to you and will be based on your situation and the resources available to you.

success steps

MAINTAINING A POSITIVE ATTITUDE

1. Keep your long-term goal in mind.
2. Negotiate and compromise.
3. Imagine you're in the workplace.
4. Weigh your options.

▶ REFLECTION QUESTIONS

- How well do you balance your priorities?
- How effective are your negotiation and compromise skills? How can you develop these communication necessities?

2

? CRITICAL THINKING QUESTIONS

2–1. What questions do you ask yourself to prioritize your responsibilities?
2–2. How do you resolve conflicting priorities?
2–3. How can you improve your communication skills?

©Image 100 Ltd.

Negotiating and compromising in a professional manner can help you collaborate with instructors to balance your commitment and responsibilities.

BARRIERS AND DETERRENTS FACING ADULT STUDENTS

Quigley (1998) and Dean (2004) elaborate on Patricia K. Cross's (1981) barriers and deterrents to adult learners. Although this research was focused on adult students, the concepts can be applied to all college students. The barriers that these educational researchers discuss include elements that pertain to your responsibilities, your perceptions of school, and processes within the school.

Cross (1981) and Kerka (1986) point out that *barriers* are in reality *deterrents*. In other words, challenges to completing your education are not barriers that prevent you from reaching your goals. Instead, they are influences that may discourage you, but not alter your course. To emphasize this point, we will use the term *deterrent* in our discussion.

SITUATIONAL DETERRENTS

Situational deterrents are those circumstances in your environment that have an effect on your ability to give your full attention to school. Examples include family-related issues such as lack of day care, transportation problems, financial issues, and home or family management concerns.

Situational deterrents are most effectively met by being aware of the resources upon which you can draw (Quigley, 1998). It is your responsibility to pursue and make arrangements for using resources that are available to you. Your school may offer a listing of resources for you to explore.

DISPOSITIONAL DETERRENTS

Dispositional deterrents are internal factors that affect your perception of or attitude toward school. Quigley (1998) identifies dispositional deterrents as having the greatest impact on learners. Consider these carefully and strive to develop an understanding of how they might influence you. Dispositional deterrents include your perceptions of school based on previous experience, your expectations, and how you perceive your abilities and level of confidence.

INSTITUTIONAL DETERRENTS

Institutional deterrents are those elements of school policy and procedure that present difficulties for adult learners. Examples include scheduling, processes that require significant time investment, or other procedures that are cumbersome and not easily completed.

It is important to keep in mind that institutional deterrents often arise from requirements over which schools have little control. Federal regulations and accreditation standards frequently require certain procedures and deadlines to be in place, and schools must abide by these in order to be in compliance. Failing to comply can hold serious consequences for a school, such as loss of accreditation or federal funding.

TYPES OF DETERRENTS TO ADULT LEARNERS

Deterrent	Definition	Examples	Solutions
Situational Deterrents	Circumstances in your environment that have an effect on your school attendance or ability to give your full attention to school	▶ Family-related issues such as lack of day care, ▶ Transportation problems, financial issues, home and family management concerns ▶ Adjusting to the college environment	▶ Student services ▶ Contacts and acquaintances ▶ Other community resources ▶ Financial aid office
Dispositional Deterrents	Internal factors that affect your perception of or attitude toward school	Your perceptions of school based on ▶ previous experience ▶ your expectations ▶ how you perceive your abilities and level of confidence	▶ Talk to your instructors. ▶ Seek support from trusted sources. ▶ Assess your perceptions. ▶ Evaluate your responses. ▶ Recognize your strengths. ▶ View needs for change as professional growth.
Institutional Barriers	Those elements of school policy and procedure that present difficulties for adult learners	Examples include ▶ scheduling ▶ processes that require significant time investment ▶ other procedures that are not designed in a way to make them easily completed	▶ Seek help from student government representatives, student focus groups, and quality circles.

Adult learners typically face various types of deterrents. Careful consideration of possible solutions to deterrents can help you stay focused and on track with your educational goals.

METHODS FOR OVERCOMING DETERRENTS

It is important to remember that although deterrents can be stressful and at times discouraging, there are methods for overcoming them. When outside concerns take temporary priority, it is important to recognize them as transient. Keep in mind that they are short-term issues within your larger goal of building your career. Remember to evaluate the most pressing priority, weigh your options, and choose the best approach for the circumstances.

2

OVERCOMING SITUATIONAL DETERRENTS

1. Remember deterrents are short-term issues.
2. Evaluate your most pressing priority.
3. Weigh your options.
4. Choose the best approach for the circumstances.

RESOURCES AND METHODS FOR OVERCOMING SITUATIONAL DETERRENTS

There are organizations and offices on and off campus that may be able to offer resources for addressing situational deterrents. Consider the following possible options.

Campus and Community Resources

Student services. Many schools have a student services department that provides support for advising, career development, and other areas related to students' professional growth. Some departments maintain lists of resources that students frequently need, including child care resources, area housing options, and other resources relevant to students' needs. Advising on a variety of topics, including adjusting to the college environment, may be available through student services. Students are responsible for contacting, evaluating, and making arrangements with the department.

Contacts and acquaintances. Word of mouth between friends and family can also be helpful. For example, friends who have children may have referrals and those with older children can be a valuable source of helpful suggestions based on experience.

Other community resources. The community in which you live can also provide an abundance of resources. For example, churches and synagogues frequently have resources for day care and other support services. Brainstorm a list of possible resources that you have available to you based on your circumstances.

Financial aid office. The financial aid office at your school has information regarding student loans, grants, and scholarships. It may also have information regarding off-campus financial resources if it does not have resources that meet your needs. Consider contacting financial aid personnel at your school if you have financial concerns, even if you believe you don't qualify for funds. Financial aid counselors are trained in identifying the best resources available for your needs and may have creative ideas that can be helpful to you.

The library. Remember the library as support source. There are numerous publications that summarize resources for a variety of financial and other topics. Ask the reference librarian for assistance in locating resources that are relevant to your needs.

Strategies for Addressing Situational Deterrents

There are also definitive actions that you can take to lessen the burden of situational deterrents. Other students also face the same dilemmas, and you may be able to create effective solutions by working with peers. Consider the following strategies.

Carpooling. Find classmates who live in your area and arrange to help each other out in the event of a transportation emergency. You might want to consider carpooling on a regular basis if it fits in with your other schedule demands. If you need to get to work immediately after class, carpooling may not be an effective option. If it does fit your schedule, carpooling can save you money and provide an opportunity to get to know your classmates.

Public transportation. It may be to your benefit to learn what public transportation is available in your area. Many mass transit systems offer discounted fare options for students who present valid school identification. Public transportation eliminates the stress of traffic and long commutes, is typically less costly than purchasing gasoline, and gives you time to read or study while someone else does the driving.

Child care co-ops. An alternative to day care providers or other child care services is a child care cooperative developed and managed by students with children. Creating a co-op requires thoughtful coordination, as you need to find a compatible mix of people who can be available at various times to be the care provider. Your student services office may be able to assist you in organizing a child care co-op.

Community child care options. In addition to home and commercial child care options, there are organizations in the community that may be a resource or offer one. For example, *M.O.P.S. (Mothers of Preschoolers)* and *Mothers and More* are organizations that advocate for families and may have suggestions for meeting child care needs.

Creative work opportunities. Financial issues are common concerns of college students. For adult learners with family responsibilities, this matter can become even more pressing. Research creative job opportunities that

Use the library and other sources available to you to research campus and community resources.

! RESOURCE BOX

EXAMPLES OF RESOURCES FOR ADDRESSING SITUATIONAL BARRIERS

- Student services
- Contacts and acquaintances
- Other community resources
- Financial aid office
- The library

2

Mass transit is one community resource that can provide a convenient and economical alternative for students.

! RESOURCE BOX

EXAMPLES OF STRATEGIES FOR ADDRESSING SITUATIONAL DETERRENTS
- Carpooling
- Public transportation
- Child care co-ops
- Community child care options
- Creative work opportunities
- Community financial resources
- Online learning options
- Use of other technology

can provide flexible hours and good income. For example, many companies rely on Internet research or data entry. These are jobs that can typically be done at home at hours that are convenient to you, provided that deadlines are met.

Community financial resources. The financial aid office at your school is the most appropriate place to start if you are seeking financial assistance. Community sources, such as your bank, are also options. Banks may be able to suggest low-interest student loans or refer you to appropriate resources. Ask the customer service department or personal bankers at your bank for more information.

Consider online learning options. Online learning can add flexibility to your education by allowing you to complete requirements according to your schedule. Research online options at your school and consider taking advantage of online learning if it is available.

Use other technology. E-mail, fax, online chat, and other technical tools have greatly facilitated communication and the exchange of information. Use technology to your advantage. For example, being able to chat online with an instructor may eliminate the need for you to make a trip in for office hours.

METHODS FOR OVERCOMING DISPOSITIONAL DETERRENTS

Dispositional deterrents are internal and are part of who you are rather than being a part of your external environment. Experiencing difficulty adjusting to the college environment (for any reason) is an example of a dispositional barrier. Addressing concerns related to these types of issues requires self-reflection and self-awareness. The following suggestions are actions you can take to gain insight into your internal process and address concerns related to dispositional deterrents.

Talk to your instructors. Quigley (1998) emphasizes the importance of communicating with your instructor regarding personal concerns. Research has shown that students who talk with their instructors regularly are more successful at persisting in school. Communicating with instructors gives them the opportunity to understand your concerns and work with you to reach a mutually agreeable solution to issues.

Seek support from trusted sources. Make a list of people in your life whom you respect and trust. Examples include clergy, relatives and friends with whom you are close, former or current instructors, and other personal and professional contacts. Reviewing problems aloud and getting feedback may help you gain insight into solving problems. Discussing your personal concerns and getting honest opinions from people you trust may help you overcome dispositional deterrents.

Assess your perceptions. Kerka (1986) emphasizes the importance of the individual's perception of his or her situation. Research suggests that deterrents have less impact on students who perceive the deterrents as obstacles that can be overcome. Evaluate your perceptions of the deterrents that you face and engage in a logical problem-solving process to arrive at solutions. Consider a brainstorming session with a trusted individual as part of the problem-solving process.

Evaluate your responses. Your responses to events in the environment are also important (Kerka, 1986). Reacting to situations in a manner that prevents you from approaching a problem in a logical and thoughtful manner is generally detrimental to overcoming deterrents that you face. For example, reacting emotionally in anger or withdrawing from a problem situation greatly reduces the opportunities for effective problem solving.

Recognize your strengths. Everyone has strengths that can be applied to their professional growth. Use feedback from others to develop an understanding of your strengths and explore ways to use them advantageously in your field. Recognizing your strengths and using them to market your skills and talents appropriately is an important part of professionalism and finding your professional niche. Ask your trusted source for feedback on your strengths.

View the need for changes as an opportunity for professional growth. Just as everyone has strengths, they also have areas of challenge and areas in which they can improve. Rather than a "weakness," consider areas of challenge a "strength gap" and set goals for professional development. Your trusted source can also provide you with insight into areas you might need to develop and help you brainstorm ideas for setting and achieving goals.

Getting feedback and advice from a trusted source can provide insight into your strengths, as well as areas to develop for your academic and professional success.

REFLECTION QUESTIONS

- How do you perceive deterrents in your environment?
- How do you respond to deterrents in your environment?

CRITICAL THINKING QUESTION

2–4. How can you monitor your perceptions and responses and change them as needed?

success steps

STEPS FOR OVERCOMING DISPOSITIONAL DETERRENTS

1. Talk to your instructors.
2. Seek support from trusted sources.
3. Assess your perceptions.
4. Evaluate your responses.
5. Recognize your strengths.
6. View the need for changes as professional growth.

apply it

Monitoring Perceptions and Responses

GOAL: *To increase your awareness of your responses to deterrents and maximize productive responses.*

STEP 1: Divide a piece of paper into three columns. In the left-hand column, write a list of the deterrents that you personally face. In the middle column, identify and describe how you react to that deterrent. For example, if your method of transportation is unreliable (the deterrent) and you react by getting angry and missing class, describe that in the middle column. In the right-hand column, record alternative reactions and solutions to the deterrent. Take the actions that you need to take to implement alternative solutions (for example, familiarizing yourself with public transportation). (Note: You can create this document electronically if you prefer.)

STEP 2: Reflect on the deterrents, responses, and alternatives that you have listed. Make it a point to be conscious of these and keep them in your awareness.

STEP 3: When you face one of your deterrents, recall your list. If you are a visual person, consider carrying the list with you as a reference. Take a few seconds to monitor your response and consider whether it is the most productive response you can make. For example, if you get angry and decide to miss class, stop and consider if this is the most helpful reaction. Consider the alternative responses and actions that you recorded.

STEP 4: Replace any nonproductive emotional response with your constructive alternative response. Note your emotional response when you take the more productive action.

STEP 5: Record your progress in a journal. Over time, you should see a change in your initial response to deterrents that you encounter. Put the journal entries in your Learning Portfolio.

METHODS FOR OVERCOMING INSTITUTIONAL DETERRENTS

Institutional deterrents may be the most difficult deterrents for students to address because some of the policies may be in place for compliance reasons and cannot be changed. However, it may be possible to streamline some procedures.

If you find policies and procedures that seem unnecessarily restrictive, first find out if they are in place for a reason, such as compliance with federal regulations or accreditation standards. If they are not, approach the situation in a professional and thoughtful manner. Demonstrate professionalism by knowing your facts and presenting them logically and through appropriate channels. The following types of student groups have traditionally addressed institutional issues:

▶ **Student government.** Some campuses have a formal student government, typically composed of elected officers and representatives whose job is to organize events, represent concerns of the student body, and serve as a liaison between students and administration. Student government representatives can be contacted regarding concerns about policies and procedures that seem unnecessarily restrictive to adult students.

▶ **Student focus groups.** If a formal student government is not available, student focus groups can be formed to research issues and develop input from the student perspective. Your school may have a procedure for initiating this process. Check with your student services department, department chair, or other administrator to ensure that you are working within acceptable boundaries. Following established protocol will add to your chances for success.

▶ **Quality circles.** Quality circles are groups that meet on a regular basis to review and monitor the school environment and to advocate for processes that contribute to quality education. Quality circles typically consist of students, faculty, and possibly administrators. Membership usually rotates so that new and different perspectives are represented.

! RESOURCE BOX

EXAMPLES OF STRATEGIES FOR ADDRESSING INSTITUTIONAL DETERRENTS
- Student government
- Student focus groups
- Quality circles

©Image 100 Ltd.

Effective verbal and nonverbal communication skills, as well as facilitation skills, are incorporated into classroom activities such as giving presentations.

success steps

HELPFUL STRATEGIES FOR ADDRESSING INSTITUTIONAL DETERRENTS

1. Research a protocol to see if it is required for compliance with regulations and standards.

2. Research the issue thoroughly.

3. Know your facts.

4. Present your case through appropriate channels.

5. Be professional and logical.

apply it

Success Resources

STEP 1: Create three columns in an electronic document or on a sheet of paper. (For ample space, use the landscape orientation for your page.) Label the columns "Situational Deterrents," "Dispositional Deterrents," and "Institutional Deterrents." Then divide each of the three columns in half. Label each pair of subcolumns "Concerns" and "Resources."

STEP 2: List the deterrents that you experience in the "Concerns" column and list potential sources for support in the "Resources" column. Note the outcomes of contacts with resources and record important contact information for future reference.

apply it

Resource Brainstorming

STEP 1: Create a group of peers who share a desire to create a resource bank for common student needs, such as day care.

STEP 2: Decide on the format for your group. You may wish to meet in person and elect a recorder for the group. One of the benefits of meeting in person, at least for the first meeting, is the positive energy generated in a face-to-face brainstorming group. A more convenient method is to create an e-mail group so that each participant receives a copy of the resource and the group can be asynchronous (you don't have to be in the same place at the same time to be effective). You may choose a combination of formats. It is important to select a format that works for the group members.

STEP 3: Share ideas and information regarding resources that group members might find helpful. Members can post needs related to long-term planning ("I need a new babysitter beginning next school term") or for more immediate concerns ("I need a babysitter for next week"). General information can also be posted ("My neighbor just started a day care, if anyone is interested").

PROFESSIONALISM AND PREPARING FOR THE WORKPLACE

Developing professional attitudes and behaviors is as important as (some would say more important than) gaining technical experience. Professionalism consists of behaviors that are acceptable in the workplace as well as how you present yourself and are perceived by coworkers and customers or clients.

ELEMENTS OF PROFESSIONALISM

Professionalism is a combination of many factors. In total, these elements provide the impression that you give to those around you. Consider how the following elements blend to convey a sense of professionalism.

Professional Presentation

Professional presentation includes appearance and dress. It also refers to the overall image as observed in a composite of behaviors such as attitude, interpersonal skills, ethics, and numerous other personal characteristics. Professional presentation can be broken down into the following components.

Personal Traits

Many personal traits contribute to one's professional presentation. Personal traits are subject to some degree of subjective interpretation, but the following traits are generally accepted as professional:

▶ **Attitude.** A professional attitude is one that is positive yet realistic and conveys a "can-do" orientation to tasks. A professional attitude communicates self-confidence with openness to growth and learning, as well as a cooperative spirit and a concern for the welfare of the group and group goals. Self-motivation and taking responsibility for oneself within the group boundaries are also part of a professional attitude.

▶ **Dependability and responsibility.** Dependability means arriving on time for class or work, being prepared, and completing projects on time. If circumstances prevent this, the professional gives ample notification and suggests alternative solutions for completing the task.

▶ **Self-management.** Self-management is the ability to be aware of one's behavior and manage it in such a way that professional

▶ REFLECTION QUESTIONS

- How do you define *professionalism*?
- What can you do in school to develop the professional skills you will need in the workplace?

2

? CRITICAL THINKING QUESTIONS

2–5. How ethical are your actions?

2–6. How can ethics and universal principles be incorporated into your daily activities?

2–7. Do you agree or disagree with the following statement? Defend your position. "How someone gets something done doesn't matter, as long as the job is accomplished and no one gets hurt."

standards are consistently met. Professionalism entails being aware of schedules and deadlines, being able to manage time and prioritize tasks, and monitoring one's performance for quality.

Ethics

Professionalism reflects an awareness of and concern for high standards of behavior, doing what is right based on universal principles. Most professions have a code of ethics that members of the profession are expected to uphold in their daily activities. Examples of universal ethics principles include honesty, fairness, and beneficence (acting for the good of another person).

Effective Communication

Effective communication means providing adequate information, ensuring that you receive adequate information to complete an assignment or task, and being able to exchange information in a variety of settings.

▶ **Group skills.** In most professional settings, the ability to work cooperatively to meet a group goal is essential. Group skills include being able to compromise, negotiate, contribute, and collaborate to build ideas and solutions.

▶ **Facilitation skills.** Facilitation skills contribute to leading effective meetings, guiding communication to reach group goals, and giving effective presentations.

▶ **Verbal communication.** Communicating effectively involves being assertive, being polite and tactful, using acceptable language, and conveying messages accurately and on time.

▶ **Nonverbal communication.** Many people believe that nonverbal communication communicates more than verbal communication. Nonverbal communication includes your facial expressions, posture, and eye contact. Nonverbal communication can convey impressions such as whether you are paying attention or showing respect.

▶ **Effective listening.** Listening is one of the more essential components of communication. Listen carefully to what others tell you and pay attention to what they are communicating nonverbally. Effective listening also involves being able to clarify to ensure understanding, receiving messages with an open and objective attitude, and demonstrating sensitivity to the emotional content of messages.

▶ **Effective written communication.** Written communication is often the first impression you make in the business world. Professional written communication demonstrates accurate grammar and spelling as well as language appropriate to the professional setting.

It includes keeping required records and documentation using accepted formats and protocols.

▶ **Diversity in communication.** Communication practices frequently vary cross-culturally and depending on the way in which an individual has been raised. Levels of assertiveness, the manner of interacting with authority figures, and the meanings of words and nonverbal gestures are examples of communication elements that can vary. As much as possible, it is important to understand the individuals with whom you're communicating and remain sensitive to their responses during your interactions with them.

Diversity Awareness

Diversity awareness is the demonstration of respect for individuals with disabilities and from different cultural groups, lifestyles, age groups, socioeconomic groups, and genders. It includes being aware of words and actions that may be offensive to others and refraining from using offensive elements in communication and other activities.

Professional Development

Professional development includes meeting the requirements of your profession, as well as taking the responsibility to maintain current knowledge in your field.

▶ **Credentialing and licensing.** You are responsible for acquiring any certification and license that is required in your field. It is your responsibility to know credentialing and continuing education requirements.

▶ **Professional conduct.** Many professions are regulated legally and have standards of practice. You are responsible for understanding these parameters and for conducting yourself accordingly. You are obligated to practice within the boundaries of your expertise and skills and refer to another professional if you are not qualified to perform a certain task. Being aware of liability issues and preventing unsafe conditions is also a professional expectation.

▶ **General business knowledge.** Professional behavior includes using technology appropriately and keeping up to date with the technical and business developments in your field. You must understand the significance of financial and marketing issues as well as administrative and management concerns and roles in daily business operations.

▶ **Lifelong learning.** Professionalism involves the ability and responsibility to remain current in your field and to be aware of

2

recent developments and new knowledge. Effective professionals recognize the need for continued education beyond school and set professional goals for their continuing development. They are able to locate and use resources effectively in order to stay current in their field.

In addition to the technical knowledge you are developing in school, also be aware of opportunities to consider and practice professional skills. These are skills that transcend subject matter and are relevant in all classes and areas of study. Think about these skills on a daily basis and increase your awareness of opportunities to practice them.

apply it

Web Research

GOAL: *To research professionalism and methods for professional development online.*

STEP 1: Conduct an Internet search using the terms "professionalism" and "professional development." (You are likely to get results from professions other than your own, but the information is usually applicable to all professionals.)

STEP 2: Bookmark or print articles that would be a good resource for understanding professionalism.

STEP 3: Share and exchange resources with classmates who are doing this activity.

apply it

Professional Development Journal

STEP 1: Select a format that you will use regularly. Some people prefer an electronic journal, while others prefer the traditional bound type. Choose the type that you will use.

STEP 2: Start by reflecting on and recording your strengths. Write about your strengths, how they can benefit you, how you can use them, and how they can contribute to your professional growth. Add observations and thoughts that are important to you.

STEP 3: Next, reflect on your "strength gaps" (challenge areas). How would you like to develop these? How can your strengths support you? Set short-term goals for developing these areas and note resources and methods for goal achievement.

STEP 4: Write in your journal at least once or twice weekly, more often when you reach a milestone or make an observation that you want to make sure you remember. Record developing strengths and new elements of yourself that you wish to develop. Review your journal regularly to see your progress.

STEP 5: Based on the entries in your journal, set goals as part of a professional development plan.

CHAPTER SUMMARY

This chapter addressed deterrents that often pose difficulties for students who are getting an education while fulfilling numerous other life responsibilities. Situational, dispositional, and institutional deterrents were discussed, and methods for addressing each of these were suggested.

The remaining chapters in *100% Student Success* provide recommendations for self-management and professional development that can support you in addressing challenges that you face during your education. Strategies suggested throughout the text can provide a foundation for sound self- management techniques that can help you keep your organization and minimize disruption from challenges that arise. As you read through the text, personalize the information provided to meet your individual needs.

POINTS TO KEEP IN MIND

In this chapter, several main points were discussed in detail:

▶ Adult learners must balance a variety of life priorities such as family, school, life management tasks, and employment.

▶ While all life priorities are important, some priorities become more pressing at times.

▶ Most instructors understand the adult student's need to balance priorities and appreciate open communication and the sincere effort on the student's part to prioritize coursework appropriately.

2

- Assess the deterrents that you face and use appropriate resources to address them.
- Develop your professional presentation, skills, and behaviors.

LEARNING OBJECTIVES REVISITED

Review the learning objectives for this chapter and rate your level of achievement for each objective using the rating scale provided. For each objective on which you do not rate yourself as a 3, outline a plan of action that you will take to fully achieve the objective. Include a time frame for this plan.

1 = did not successfully achieve objective

2 = understand what is needed, but need more study or practice

3 = achieved learning objective thoroughly

	1	2	3
Define issues and barriers and deterrents common to adult students.	☐	☐	☐
Identify methods of addressing barriers and deterrents and locate resources for addressing them.	☐	☐	☐
Describe professionalism and professional conduct and demonstrate it through actions and behavior.	☐	☐	☐
Devise a professional development plan for transition to the workplace.	☐	☐	☐

Steps to Achieve Unmet Objectives

Steps   Due Date

1. _____   _____

2. _____   _____

3. _____   _____

4. _____   _____

SUGGESTED ITEMS FOR LEARNING PORTFOLIO

- Reflection and Critical Thinking Questions: Include your written responses to these questions. Use them to review your development over time.

▶ Monitoring Perceptions and Responses: This activity helps you monitor your responses to deterrents that you face and is intended to help you develop more productive responses as well as your resource options.

▶ Success Resources: This activity is intended to help you identify deterrents that you face and identify multiple resources for addressing them. Consider adding the results of the Resource Brainstorming Activity to this list.

▶ Professional Development Journal and Professional Development Plan: The journal is meant to help you reflect on your experiences, monitor your progress, and set goals for future development.

▶ Web Research: Compile your resources from your Web research and use them as a reference for your professional growth and development.

REFERENCES

Cross, K. P. (1981). *Adults as Learners.* San Francisco: Jossey-Bass.

Dean, G. J. (2004). An introduction to adult learners: Nothing is for sure [Electronic version]. *Fieldnotes for ABLE Staff.* Commonwealth of Pennsylvania. Retrieved January 31, 2005, from the Pennsylvania Department of Education, Bureau of Adult Basic and Literacy Education Web site: http://www.able.state.pa.us/able/lib/able/fieldnotes04/fn04adultlearner.pdf

Kerka, S. (1986). Deterrents to participation in adult education. ERIC Digest No. 56 Retrieved June 22, 2006 from http://www.eric.ed.gov/ERICWebPortal/Home.portal?_nfpb=true&eric_viewStyle=list&ERICExtSearch_SearchValue_0=kerka&ERICExtSearch_SearchType_0=au&pageSize=10&eric_displayNtriever=false&eric_displayStartCount=51&_pageLabel=RecordDetails&objectId=0900000b801b1e44&accno=ED275889

Imel, S. (2001). Adult learners in postsecondary education [Electronic version]. Clearinghouse on Adult, Career, and Vocational Education (ACVE), Center on Education and Training for Employment, The Ohio State University College of Education Columbus, OH. Retrieved August 18, 2005, from http://www.cete.org/acve/docgen.asp?tbl=pab&ID=107

Quigley, B. A. (1998). The first three weeks: A critical time for motivation [Electronic version]. *Focus on Basics, 2,* A. Retrieved January 31, 2005, from The National Center for the Study of Adult Learning and Literacy Web site: http://gseweb.harvard.edu/~ncsall/fob/1998/quigley.htm

©Image 100 Ltd.

CHAPTER OUTLINE

Functions of the Brain in Learning

Learning Styles and Type Preferences

Active Learning

Successful Skills for Learning

Technology in the Classroom

3 Learning Strategies

LEARNING OBJECTIVES

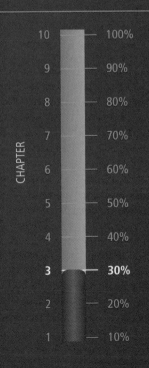

By the end of this chapter, you will achieve the following objectives:

▶ Define *active learning* and *teamwork*.

▶ Explain the impact of the functions of the brain on the learning experience.

▶ Discuss the various learning styles.

▶ Explain the importance of determining your preferred learning style.

▶ Describe an effective study environment.

▶ Explain how to improve reading skills.

▶ Describe methods used for effective note taking.

▶ Discuss methods for studying and learning math effectively.

▶ Discuss methods for studying and taking tests effectively.

▶ Discuss methods to minimize test anxiety.

▶ Explain the differences between preparing for an objective exam versus an essay exam.

▶ Explain the basic principles of using selected memory enhancement techniques.

▶ Describe a hybrid course.

3

TOPIC SCENARIO

Lynn, Dale, Drew, and Bryce have always been a cohesive and successful leadership team at the business of Schmidt and Schmidt. As team leaders of the various departments at Schmidt and Schmidt, these four individuals have accomplished a variety of team projects. In addition to successfully managing cohesive work groups, the managers work effectively as a team to complete project goals and fulfill responsibilities. Upper management at Schmidt and Schmidt has recognized this leadership team for its strong efforts and effective team management and asked Lynn, Dale, Drew, and Bryce to provide a presentation detailing their strategies for their success. The points they presented included the following:

▶ Understanding and respecting team members' individual learning styles

▶ Understanding and respecting team members' interpersonal styles and preferences

▶ Communicating consistently and accurately within and between work teams

▶ Recognizing and honoring both team and individual accomplishments as projects are completed

Eventually, the need for a fifth team leader became apparent and the four members of the leadership team were asked to participate in the hiring process. Based on this scenario, answer the following questions:

▶ How can understanding and respecting your own learning preference contribute to your success as a team member?

▶ How can understanding your interpersonal style and preference contribute to your success as a team member?

▶ Why is recognition of both team and individual accomplishments important? How does recognition contribute to productivity and organizational goals?

▶ When considering a recent college graduate, how might the four team leaders be able to assess the candidate's abilities in the skills desired prior to hiring?

▶ As a college student, what can you do while you are in school to understand and develop the learning and interpersonal skills that will be important on work teams?

FUNCTIONS OF THE BRAIN IN LEARNING

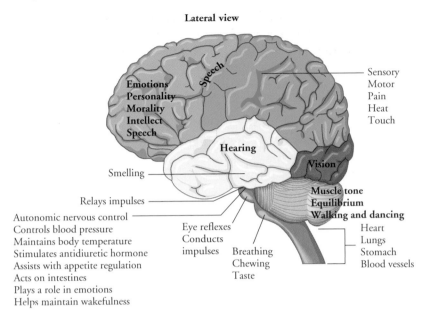

Different parts of the brain control various aspects of behavior and learning.

Over the years, research has been conducted to understand how the brain functions and how individuals learn. For years it has been known that elements such as stress, anxiety, and lack of sleep can affect the ability to learn. To further understand the effects that the human brain can have on learning, Renate Nummela Caine and Geoffrey Caine (Maine Support Network, 1997) proposed principles of "brain-based learning." These principles help to explain how the brain functions and the impact that these functions can have on learning experiences. Some of these principles are listed here.

▶ Due to the complexity of the brain, learning is best accomplished by utilizing a variety of learning methods and techniques.

▶ Physiological reactions of the body, including responses to stress, fatigue, poor nutrition, and illness, affect the brain's functions and learning capacity. Individual development rates also affect learning.

▶ The brain is constantly trying to find meaning in experiences and automatically reacts to surrounding stimuli. Learning occurs when the environment is one that is secure and consistent but also allows new challenges and the discovery of new information.

▶ Information is better learned when it is well organized. If information doesn't make sense, the brain naturally tries to organize the information into some sort of pattern. Well-organized information

3

allows you to focus on the material rather than attempting to try and make sense of information that is unclear or seemingly unrelated.

▶ Emotions play a critical role in learning. Learning is largely dependent on how you feel about yourself (self-esteem), your attitude toward the material, your preconceived ideas, and how you are responding to the environment on a given day. Emotions also affect the ability to memorize and recall information. A school and classroom environment that provides emotional support through mutual respect and acceptance will foster learning.

▶ The brain responds to all stimuli in some way. Learning occurs through use of both subtle and distinct methods. For example, you respond to visual aids as well as to the enthusiasm that the instructor exhibits about the information being presented.

▶ Learning occurs unconsciously and consciously. In addition to the information presented in class, you are also receiving cues from the human and physical environments. While you may not consciously attend to the more subtle environmental cues, they have an influence on your learning.

▶ The brain remembers information in at least two ways. The spatial memory system occurs without a conscious effort to remember information. For example, remembering that a streetlight is at the end of the block by the school is something that is automatically placed in the memory. It didn't have to be intentionally memorized. Experiencing or seeing something new motivates this system into action. Another system in the brain stores information such as facts and skills and is dependent on rote memory and repetition. Learning facts and skills should occur through use of both memory systems. Remembering occurs more readily when learning involves a variety of activities such as demonstrations, projects, field trips, visual imagery, stories, drama, and so forth. Make use of both memory systems by taking advantage of various activities offered in your classes that involve all your senses in the learning process.

▶ REFLECTION QUESTION

• What did you learn regarding the impact your brain has on your learning?

? CRITICAL THINKING QUESTION

3–1. What is your reaction to the following statement? "There is too much emphasis on how the brain functions when it comes to learning. It isn't as complex as some people make it out to be."

LEARNING STYLES AND TYPE PREFERENCES

Understanding your preferred learning style can contribute to optimal learning. Each person has a preferred way of learning information. For example, some students learn and retain information most effectively when it is portrayed in illustrations (visual learning style) while other students learn most effectively by listening to a lecture (auditory learning style). Others may learn best by engaging in activity and trying it out (kinesthetic learners) and some may learn best by building, writing, or manipulating objects or tools in some other way (tactile learners).

You may find that learning new material is easiest for you when you use your preferred learning style. Being able to create methods based on your learning style to support your studying will benefit you throughout school as well as in the workplace. Letting instructors and employers know your preferred learning style will support them in helping you to develop your skills.

It is important to remember, however, that it is of value to you to be able to learn using all styles, and it is to your advantage to develop your skills in all learning areas. Success in your academic studies and as a professional requires not only an understanding of your preferred learning style but also calls for the ability to incorporate other learning style models into your skill set. For example, even though an individual might naturally be more comfortable using illustrations, it is advantageous to be able to learn techniques by listening to a verbal explanation.

Learning styles are commonly categorized into auditory, visual, tactile (touch), and kinesthetic (movement and doing) modes. Figure 3–1 illustrates these four learning styles and gives examples of activities that support each. Remember that it is important to learn using all of these modes; however, you may be most successful in learning new information using the mode that comes to you most naturally.

There are other models that describe how individuals learn, including Kolb's Learning Style Model, the Herrmann Brain Dominance Instrument (HBDI), and the Felder-Silverman Learning Style Model. The Myers-Briggs Type Indicator (MBTI) is considered to be a scientifically valid instrument for determining an individual's preferences for processing information on a daily basis (Pelley, 2002). Although not a learning model per se, the MBTI can provide an individual with insight into how to interact with his or her environment in a way that supports learning.

You are encouraged to explore other learning models to support your awareness of your learning style.

REFLECTION QUESTIONS

- What is your preferred learning style?
- How can you improve in utilizing the other learning styles to accomplish your academic goals?

? CRITICAL THINKING QUESTIONS

3–2. What is your response to the following statement? "Knowing your learning style can assist in both academic and professional success."

3–3. What specific questions might you ask to discover an individual's preferred learning style?

apply it

Learning Models

GOAL: To develop a better understanding regarding your own personal learning style preference.

STEP 1: Conduct an Internet search using "learning styles" as your search term.

continued

3

continued

STEP 2: Compile a print or electronic file of articles pertaining to various learning models. Consider how each applies to your individual learning style. Complete learning inventories and use other tools that you find in your research.

STEP 3: An alternate activity is for each individual in the class to research one learning model. Provide copies of the articles or e-mail links of your findings to fellow group members so that each concludes the activity with a variety of resources.

STEP 4: Consider placing your resources in your Learning Portfolio.

LEARNING STYLES AND SUPPORTING ACTIVITIES

Learning Style	Sensory Modality	Activity Examples
		Activities that are likely to
If your style is . . .	You learn best using . . .	support your learning are . . .
Auditory	▶ The sense of hearing ▶ Verbal information	▶ Lectures ▶ Discussion ▶ Recordings ▶ Reciting aloud ▶ Reading (although it uses visual sense) may be effective because of its verbal nature
Visual	▶ The visual sense ▶ Diagrammed information	▶ Illustrations ▶ Pictures ▶ Visualizing ▶ Charts ▶ Diagrams ▶ Written instructions
Tactile	▶ Touching ▶ "Hands on" activity	▶ Writing ▶ Diagramming information yourself ▶ Putting something together
Kinesthetic	▶ Participation ▶ Trying before learning	▶ "Jumping right in" ▶ Experiential learning ▶ Field trips ▶ Active involvement ▶ Laboratory exercises

FIGURE 3–1.   Learning Style and Activity Chart. By identifying your preferred learning style, you can select activities from which you will learn most effectively. Even though you probably have one preferred style, It is to your benefit to learn from all types of activities.

ACTIVE LEARNING

As pointed out in the last section, there are various ways that people learn. The traditional and primary method of teaching in the academic environment is lecture. Advancements have been made in understanding the need to incorporate active learning into the classroom as a way to engage students in the learning process. Active learning involves practicing a specific skill, reflecting on its effectiveness, and practicing again to incorporate changes and improvements, as opposed to passively listening to a lecture. Active learning not only makes learning more enjoyable but can also appeal to all types of learning styles by incorporating elements such as problem solving, formulating and answering questions, discussing, debating, and brainstorming (Felder & Brent, 2003). Activities can include working in teams to solve problems and complete projects or working independently on developing materials such as learning portfolios or journals.

TEAMWORK IN THE CLASSROOM

Depending on individual preference, the ability to work in teams may not be a comfortable skill but is one that must be developed for both academic and employment success. What is teamwork? The *American Heritage Dictionary* defines *teamwork* as "cooperative effort by the members of a group or team to achieve a common goal." Learning how to work with others requires individuals to look beyond individual goals and work toward achieving the common goal in a way that benefits all team members. Successful completion of group projects requires the group to become a cohesive team. Successful formation of a cohesive team requires agreement on a common goal, effective use of individual skills within the group, and effective communication in order to include all team members and resolve conflict (NDT Resource Center, 2001).

Working in teams supports the exchange of diverse ideas and supports the development of interpersonal and cooperative skills needed in the workplace.

success steps

EFFECTIVE TEAMWORK

1. Decide on a group or team goal.
2. Use individual talents and experiences in a collaborative effort to achieve a balanced blend of talent to meet the group goal.
3. Balance individual and team needs and communicate clearly about both.
4. Address and resolve conflict as soon as possible.
5. Involve all participants in decisions.
6. Emphasize commitment to the successful achievement of the team goal.

It is the responsibility of each student to contribute to the success of group activities by learning how to be an effective team member. Understanding how you best relate to others and how you process information from your surroundings will contribute to understanding how you can best contribute to the group. For example, if you know that you tend to process information from the environment before speaking up or acting on it, you and group members can be aware of your participation style and how you can best contribute to the team.

At times, students don't work together effectively to achieve success. Understanding the signs that may indicate a lack of team cooperation provides the opportunity to address issues and improve team function. David Pucel and Rosemary Fruehling, in their book *Working in Teams,* list the following characteristics that indicate an ineffective team (Pucel & Fruehling, 1997):

- Failure to understand the group goal
- Domination of more reserved group members by more aggressive members
- Fear of expressing thoughts openly and honestly
- Fear of disagreement or conflict
- Lack of respect for others' perspectives and opinions
- Lack of interest and attention
- Decisions reached by a few while other members disagree
- Discussions that are out of control or dominated by the leader
- Unwillingness to discuss team progress or consider group processes
- Unwillingness of members to share personal feelings about the working of the team
- Unwillingness of members to complete team tasks

If students do not form cohesive teams when working on group projects, grades can often be affected. The classroom offers an environment that allows students to develop their teamwork abilities.

SUCCESSFUL SKILLS FOR LEARNING

Academic success is achieved through a variety of traditional learning activities, such as reading and note taking. Students who excel academically have developed efficient note-taking, reading, and test-taking skills in addition to participating effectively in classroom activities. The following suggestions for effective note taking, creating a positive study environment, and

REFLECTION QUESTIONS

- In what classroom activities are you most comfortable?
- If group activities are challenging for you, what can you do to improve your comfort level and group skills?

CRITICAL THINKING QUESTION

3–4. What is your reaction to the following statements? "I wish we didn't have to work in teams. I can be much more successful at accomplishing goals if I work alone."

developing reading skills are based on recommendations from the Middlebury College Office of Learning Resources (n.d.).

NOTE TAKING

The ability to take effective notes during lecture is essential to the success of college students. Thorough and accurate notes provide you with the information you need to study effectively. You can use your notes according to your learning style by translating notes into a diagram (visual learners), reciting them into a tape recorder and listening to the playback (auditory learner), or applying the notes to an activity (kinesthetic learner). Regardless of how you use the notes, note taking is the vehicle commonly used for obtaining information in class. Consequently, effective note taking is a skill that is important to learn and develop. Skills of listening and interpreting information accurately and quickly are important. For example, a common belief is that the instructor's word must be written down verbatim, but it is acceptable and more efficient to write down main themes and ideas. The following are additional suggestions for making note taking more effective and easier to accomplish:

▶ Position yourself for optimal hearing and seeing. If it is easier to hear and see by sitting near the front and center, then do so. Avoid areas such as doorways or windows, where distractions are more likely to occur. Avoid sitting next to friends who might also be a distraction. Taking meaningful notes that will be easily understood at a later study time requires full concentration.

▶ You may choose to use a word-processing program to record notes on a laptop computer. Use double or triple spacing and print your notes in black ink.

▶ If you use a notebook, make sure to purchase one that lies flat and is easily kept in order. Some students choose to have a separate notebook for each course; others choose to go with something like a three-ring binder with dividers. Choose a style that is convenient for you and that you will use. Organization of notes may be accomplished more easily with wide-lined paper and with an organization system such as a binder or notebook with pockets that allows you to add documents.

▶ When taking notes, write down main ideas with some details. Avoid writing down what the person is saying word for word.

▶ Leave white space for later additions.

▶ Be an active listener. Write down your questions as they come up and follow up to get the answers.

3

▌ Review your notes and reword as needed. If time permits, it may be helpful for some individuals (especially tactile learners) to rewrite notes as a learning tool.

▌ Add drawings and diagrams to illustrate concepts. This method is helpful for students who are visual learners.

There are numerous note-taking systems, such as the Cornell Method. Reading systems often have a note-taking component. One of these is SQR4, which stands for Survey, Question, Read, Record, Recite, Review. It is a systematic method that recommends overviewing the material, noting questions about it, reading it in thorough detail, recording notes, and reviewing the data. You are encouraged to explore various note-taking systems and select one that supports your learning.

success steps

TAKING EFFECTIVE NOTES

1. Select a method of note taking (electronic or traditional) that is best suited to your needs and preferences. For example, use a laptop computer, a single notebook divided into sections, or a spiral-bound notebook for each subject.

2. Record main ideas and enough details to allow you to fill in the remaining information later. Avoid trying to write down verbatim what the instructor says.

3. Leave space to go back to and fill in additional details while you are studying.

4. Write down questions as you think of them.

5. Review and rewrite your notes.

6. Add diagrams and drawings to illustrate concepts.

7. Use recommended note-taking methods, such as the Cornell Method.

THE STUDY ENVIRONMENT

Effective study habits will minimize distractions and maximize your benefit from studying. Study habits vary individually, and you will need to consider what is most effective for you based on your preferences and style. Consider the following suggestions:

▌ **Have a consistent study area.** Create a permanent place for your study area. Let other household members know that this is your area

Study in an environment that is organized and free of distractions so you can focus. Effective study habits contribute to academic success.

and ask that they respect the area by leaving it undisturbed. Your permanent study area should be one that promotes concentration and minimizes the likelihood of interruptions.

▶ **Apply organizational techniques.** Reflect on the organizational skills that were introduced in Chapter 1. In addition, organize your physical space by grouping supplies and materials. Doing so will not only make them easier to find, but you will know when you need to replenish supplies, and you will avoid last-minute panic. Keep necessary tools for studying in this area so that time is not wasted locating pens, paper, and other supplies. Avoid taking these study supplies for other tasks.

▶ **Make a healthy physical environment.** Minimize fatigue and eye strain by ensuring that you have adequate lighting and seating that promotes good posture and ergonomically sound positioning. Ensure that the study environment is quiet and at a comfortable temperature. Position your computer at a level that avoids neck strain.

▶ **Avoid distractions.** Commit to studying when you are in your area. Avoid the temptation to answer the telephone or doorbell. Reserve special family time so that your children and spouse don't feel neglected and are more apt to honor your study time.

▶ **Consider alternative locations.** In some situations, such as when numerous roommates are present in a household, setting up a home study environment may not be possible. If this is the case, another location may be your best choice. The school and public libraries are examples of other options.

▶ **Know your personal cycles.** Determine your most productive study time. For example, some people are most alert and productive during the early morning, while others have more energy at night. Pay attention to your biological cycles and use your time management skills to develop a schedule appropriate for you. Consider when you think best and when you are the most alert. Determine the time of day when other activities are least likely to compete for your time.

▶ **Define clear goals.** Know what you want to accomplish in each study session. Use the time management skills you learned in Chapter 1 to prioritize each task.

▶ **Take breaks.** Minimize fatigue and maximize concentration by taking breaks. A good rule of thumb is to work for 1½ hours and than rest for 20 to 30 minutes. Achieve a balance between breaks and studying. Use study time wisely to achieve complete tasks and meet your goals for each study session.

3

success steps

DEVELOPING AN EFFECTIVE STUDY ENVIRONMENT

1. Have a consistent study area.

2. Apply organizational techniques to your study habits and space.

3. Create a healthy physical environment that includes ample lighting, ergonomically sound furniture arrangements, and a comfortable room temperature.

4. Avoid distractions by turning off the phone, avoiding the doorbell, and asking family members and roommates to avoid interrupting you.

5. Consider an alternative study location, such as the library, if home cannot be made distraction free.

6. Study at the time of day when you are most focused, alert, and productive.

7. Have clearly defined goals for each study session.

8. Take a 20- to 30-minute break for every hour and a half spent studying.

READING SKILLS

College courses typically require significant reading, and developing reading skills can significantly impact your academic success. Reading can be difficult for a number of reasons, including a lack of exposure to reading, poor eyesight, or reading techniques that are not as efficient as they could be. Reading skills can frequently be improved using various techniques. To improve reading skills, consider the following guidelines:

▶ **Read for concepts.** Avoid reading every word. Instead, learn to find the words that are meaningful and build ideas. It may be helpful to take short notes and record any question that you have on important concepts.

▶ **Get an overview.** Skim through the reading assignment to determine the main idea and locate significant parts that will require more careful reading. After skimming, go back and reread the areas that need more attention and that enhance your understanding of the content.

▶ **Quiz yourself.** Ask yourself questions on the material that you have read. Go back and review the material on which you had difficulty answering questions. If studying with others is effective for you, find a partner and quiz each other.

3

▶ **Mark important points.** Highlight important content that you will need to know. Use another color to highlight information that requires further attention and study.

▶ **Use a variety of activities.** In addition to reading, use the material and concepts that you are learning. Test yourself, review, organize related concepts and facts into categories, master the technical terms and formulas, and think of ways to apply the concepts to practical situations.

▶ **Direct your attention.** Some parts of the reading assignment may not require as much attention as others. Direct your focus and attention to areas that require greater concentration.

▶ **Use recommended reading systems.** Consider researching and utilizing a reading system, such as SQR4, which (as mentioned previously) includes a note-taking component.

▶ **Use campus resources.** Investigate and use campus resources that are available to you. Learning resource centers, learning labs, and student advisors are examples of resources commonly available to students.

▶ **Use various reading speeds.** Use different reading speeds depending on the goal of your reading. Getting the general idea of a piece may require rapid skimming, as might material with which you are familiar. Conversely, unfamiliar material or material that is more difficult typically requires more focused reading at a slower rate. Modify your reading pace according to your needs and the material.

---

success steps

GETTING THE MOST FROM YOUR READING

1. Read for concepts rather than reading every word.

2. Skim the material first for an overview and to get the general idea.

3. Quiz yourself over the material that you have read.

4. Highlight information to help you learn. Use one color for important points and another color for information that you need to review.

5. Use various activities to reinforce your learning. Summarize, make diagrams, and apply the information to practical situations.

6. Direct your attention to areas in which you need the most study and review.

continued

3

? CRITICAL THINKING QUESTION

3–5. How would you respond to the following statements made by a classmate? "There are so many books we have to read for this class, I don't know how I am going to make it through. I am already so far behind in my reading I just don't think I will pass."

continued

7. Use effective reading methods, such as SQR4, to organize the material.

8. Take advantage of campus resources, such as reading labs and resource centers.

9. Vary your reading speed according to the information. Skim familiar information quickly and read more complex, unfamiliar material at a slower rate.

STUDYING MATH

Mathematics often requires study skills that differ from those needed for more verbal subjects. Active learning and doing are especially important in mastering math concepts. The following suggestions for facilitating studying and test taking in math are summarized from tips provided by the Saint Louis University Department of Mathematics and Computer Science (1993).

▶ **Actively participate.** Active learning is an important component of succeeding in math classes. Mathematical concepts are most effectively understood when they are used to solve problems. Assignments are intended to provide practice in using math concepts, so completion of homework is essential to your success. If you have questions about a step in a problem, write it down and follow up with the instructor. Try other problems using the same concepts to see if doing a different problem increases your understanding, as sometimes a slightly different perspective will help. Take responsibility for your learning by asking questions in class to clarify confusing concepts and asking questions of the instructor during office hours.

▶ **Remember that math concepts are cumulative.** Math concepts build on one another. What you learn this week is the foundation for what will be taught next week. For this reason, attending class consistently, doing all assignments, and ensuring that you understand every concept are critical components of success. Making it a point to see the relationship between concepts can be helpful. Some concepts will connect with others. Give yourself time to understand the relationships between concepts. If you aren't quite sure you understand during class time, do the homework, reread the material, and see if the next day's class makes it clearer.

◗ **Make use of all types of assignments.** You are likely to encounter various types of problems, which require diverse skills. For example, you may need to memorize formulas and complete repetitive exercises to reinforce your learning. Other problems may require you to apply what you have learned to practical situations. Understand the purpose of each type of assignment and consider how it fits into the "big picture."

◗ **Recognize differences between high school and college math.** College math courses tend to cover more material in less time and tests tend to cover more material. Homework may be assigned for your practice and benefit and may not be collected or graded by the instructor. This difference places even greater emphasis on the importance of keeping up with the class, asking questions to clarify confusing information, and taking responsibility for your performance.

◗ **Seek additional help if needed.** If you need additional help, seek resources such as a tutor or the learning resource center on your campus. Seek help as soon as you see that you need it to avoid falling behind. Do not procrastinate or skip class to avoid stress related to class, as this will only compound the difficulty.

success steps

STEPS FOR SOLVING MATH PROBLEMS

Step 1: Understand what the problem is asking you to solve. Read through and think about the entire problem.

Step 2: Draw on what you know to select techniques to solve the problem.

Step 3: Organize the techniques that you identify into a plan to solve the problem.

Step 4: Execute your plan.

Step 5: Review your answer and check your work. Consider how you might use the same techniques to solve other problems.

TEST TAKING

The ability to take tests successfully is a required skill for students in college as well as in many careers, for professional licensure or certification. Understanding how to prepare effectively for tests and how to take tests effectively can increase your success and relieve any test anxieties.

Preparation for an exam should not begin the night before the exam but should be a process that has been incorporated into your study habits on a

◗ REFLECTION QUESTIONS

• Do you think you have ever had test anxiety? If so, when? Why do you think you were anxious? What did you do to try and relieve your anxiety?

• How good are you at taking exams? How might you be able to improve?

daily basis. Devote a part of your daily study schedule to reviewing material in preparation for upcoming exams. Repetition and building on information as you receive it over time are effective long-term study techniques. Completing assignments and reading the material daily also contribute to the ongoing preparation for an exam. Consider every assignment and project as preparation for exams. It is especially important to record any questions that arise during this process and follow through with the instructor to get your questions answered.

How you prepare for an exam is partly dependent on whether the exam will be an objective or essay-type exam. Determine the range of information that will be included on the test and types of questions that will be asked. Ask your instructor for this information if it has not been provided.

The two main types of questions asked on exams are objective questions (multiple choice, true/false, and matching) and essay questions, which require a written response of a specified length. Objective questions typically require a response that demonstrates knowledge and comprehension of facts. Essay questions usually require you to be more analytical and to synthesize and answer by relating several concepts.

Consider the following strategies for *preparing for an objective exam*:

▶ The technique of formulating questions and answers from course material is an effective method. If you benefit from studying with classmates, this is an effective technique for study groups.

▶ Focus on facts and objective information such as definitions, theorems, and formulas. Using flash cards with a term or question on one side and the definition or answer on the reverse side is an effective method for learning factual material. For example, if you are learning various theorems, you might write the theorem on one side of the flash card and its use on the other. This technique can be used individually or in a study group.

▶ Ensure that you have included all information from textbooks and class handouts. If your instructor has indicated that information from other media (such as videos, CDs, or Web sites) will be covered, be sure to review these as well. Find out how to gain access to the media if access is not readily available.

▶ If your objective exam includes calculations such as those common in classes such as math, chemistry, or other applied courses, it is important to drill yourself on the types of problems on which you will be tested. Practice is the key to mastering applied subjects requiring problem solving.

Preparing for essay exams requires different approaches, as you will need to analyze concepts and synthesize them into a cogent response to the question. It is also important to recall the study strategies for objective tests in order to have accurate information from which to draw in answering the essay questions. You need correct information as the basis for the responses that you will develop in an essay test. Consider the following strategies for *preparing for an essay-type exam:*

▶ As you read course material, pay attention to the relationships between concepts and ideas. Consider the conclusions you can draw from the relationships that you discover.

▶ Develop a system for showing the relationships between concepts. For example, a concept map can effectively illustrate the relationships between ideas. Likewise, concepts written on index cards can be arranged in a variety of ways to illustrate relationships and to formulate a premise for supporting an idea or thesis.

▶ Practice expressing yourself by writing the relationships and conclusions that you find. Use concepts from your English classes to organize your response to include a major thesis and supporting themes. Include an effective introduction and conclusion. If your response is one that appropriately includes your opinion or assessment of a situation, support your opinion with accurate and logical facts and reasoning.

For any type of exam, certain strategies can help you make the most of the time you have to complete the questions. Much of successful test taking is budgeting your time, having a general idea of what is on the test, and reading thoroughly. Refer to the "Success Steps" for detailed tips on successful test taking.

success steps

TIPS FOR SUCCESSFUL TEST TAKING

1. Know the amount of time you have to complete the test. Divide the total amount of time that you have by the number of questions on the test to get a general idea of approximately how much time you can spend on each question. Of course, some questions will take longer than others, but this method will help you gauge your time effectively.

2. Read through the entire test. Reading through the test will provide you with an overview and general picture of what the test entails. This will also help you to effectively allocate your time to each of the questions.

continued

3

continued

3. Read directions carefully. Misunderstanding test directions can cause you to lose points by using the wrong approach to the questions. Ensure that you understand the directions and request clarification as needed.

4. Answer the questions that you know first. Doing so gets them "out of the way" so that you can spend more time on items that require more concentration and time. Answering the questions you know may offer insight into more difficult questions.

5. Pay attention to clues that will help you answer more difficult questions. Sometimes, answering one question will provide clues to the answers to other questions.

6. Answer all questions. It is usually to your advantage to answer all questions in some way. Even if you are unsure of the entire answer, use the information you do know to provide an answer. Doing so will increase your chances for at least partial credit.

Preparing carefully, studying, and getting adequate sleep and nutrition will support improved test performance.

©Digital Vision

Individuals who experience test anxiety can use the following additional techniques for minimizing anxiety before an exam:

1. Follow the guidelines for preparing for and taking exams. Effective preparation and an organized approach to test taking can significantly reduce anxiety.

2. Take care of yourself. Get a full night's rest before the exam. Fatigue can increase anxiety and reduce effective thinking skills.

3. Review reasonably the night before the exam. Avoid cramming. If you have kept up with your assignments and ongoing review, you won't need to cram at the last minute. Review, quiz yourself, and get sufficient rest. Ensure that you get sufficient sleep and avoid using any type of sleeping aid that could leave you drowsy in the morning.

4. If you believe that you need additional review, allow time in your morning schedule to arrive at school early and review your material. Or, if you prefer, review at home. Budget your time

so that you are not rushed and can arrive at the test feeling composed and relaxed.

5. Eat a healthy meal before a test. Doing so will maximize your energy and concentration.

apply it

Study Techniques

GOAL: To apply study techniques to your learning experience.

STEP 1: Make an honest assessment of your study and test-taking skills. Pinpoint specific areas in which you would like to develop your skills. For example, you may discover that you need to improve your note-taking skills in your literature class. Note area(s) for improvement as specifically as possible.

STEP 2: Research methods for making changes in the areas you identify. For example, if you need to improve your note-taking skills, conduct an Internet search using "note taking" as your search term. Consider the methods mentioned in this chapter (the Cornell Method for note taking and the SQR4 method for reading comprehension).

STEP 3: Set specific goals and create a plan for applying what you learn to your assignments and class work.

STEP 4: Assess your progress and adjust your goals as needed to continue your improvement.

MEMORY TECHNIQUES

Knowledge for the exam is important, but remembering the material from classes in preparation for a career is even more critical. Future professional success requires you to recall information learned in the academic environment as well as to apply it to practical situations. Here are several methods that can be used in aiding your memory:

> **Imagery.** To use imagery to recall important information, associate an image with the information you are trying to memorize. For example, if you are learning a chemistry formula, you might visualize the corresponding steps in a lab experiment. If you are memorizing the steps in repairing an engine, visualize yourself actually working on the engine. This technique can be adapted to a wide variety of fields and activities.

> **Association.** Associating information with things that you already know puts information in a context and links it to something that

3

REFLECTION QUESTIONS

- How do you memorize information? Do you use different methods depending on what you are trying to memorize?
- Do you think the method(s) you use work best, or would trying some other methods be helpful?

is already familiar. For example, if you are learning a new computer program, associating its functionality with another similar program can jog your memory as well as allow you to highlight the differences between the two.

▶ **Mnemonics.** Mnemonics are verbal reminders that make use of rhymes, familiar tunes, and acronyms to help you remember information. A well-known mnemonic is "Roy G. Biv," which stands for the order of the colors of the rainbow: <u>r</u>ed, <u>o</u>range, <u>y</u>ellow, green, <u>b</u>lue, <u>i</u>ndigo, and <u>v</u>iolet. You may find mnemonics that are commonly used in your field, or you might find it effective to create your own mnemonics.

The tools and techniques suggested here are only a few suggestions for memory enhancement. Consider conducting further research to find the memory tool that works best for you. Memory techniques can be found in a variety of resources, including books, articles, journals, and on the Internet.

apply it

Memory Techniques

GOAL: *To gain further understanding of and appreciation for memory techniques.*

STEP 1: Conduct a search on the Web to locate various memory techniques. Use "memorization techniques" or "improving memory" as the search terms.

STEP 2: Write a brief report on what Web sites were researched, the memory techniques found, and opinions regarding the effectiveness of each technique.

STEP 3: Consider placing this worksheet in your Learning Portfolio.

©Digital Vision

Computers and technology are becoming a major learning tool in the classroom and have made the hybrid class possible.

TECHNOLOGY IN THE CLASSROOM

The college classroom continues to evolve as technology advances. Internet research has become a more common requirement for the completion of in-class and homework activities. Although as of 2002 only about

1% of the U.S. population had taken a course online, many schools are continuing to develop methods to integrate technology into the classroom (Fryer, 2001–2002). One method that is gaining popularity is the hybrid course. Hybrid courses incorporate both online and classroom activities. The online portion of a hybrid class typically provides information that lends itself to the online format, while the classroom component offers hands-on activities. Utilizing the Internet for accessing lecture notes and PowerPoint presentations allows students more flexibility in completing class requirements. "The goal of hybrid courses is to join the best features of in-class teaching with the best features of online learning to promote active independent learning and reduce class seat time" (Garnham & Kaleta, 2002, p. 1).

There are a variety of different technology options, known as *platforms,* that are used to create and facilitate a course online. These include:

▶ Blackboard

▶ E-college

▶ WebCT

Both students and faculty need to learn how to make this type of classroom effective. Students who are considering or taking a course with an online component should be aware that the online component requires as much effort and time as "on-ground" (in-class) learning. Online course components require participation in online discussion, responses to questions, submission of online assignments, and active learning projects. The ability to manage time and organize both online and on-ground components is essential to your success in a hybrid course.

REFLECTION QUESTIONS

- How might you benefit from taking a hybrid course?
- What concerns might you have in taking a hybrid course?

? CRITICAL THINKING QUESTION

3–6. How would you respond to the following statement? "Online learning is the wave of the future."

CHAPTER SUMMARY

This chapter provided information directed at supporting your learning and improving your study skills and habits. Understanding various learning models and the importance of understanding your preferred learning style were emphasized. You were also encouraged to develop learning styles that may be less comfortable to you but that can enhance your learning. Study skills, test-taking methods, and memorization techniques were also introduced. To gain optimally from this information, you are encouraged to understand and develop your learning styles and create study habits and routines that support them. Study techniques that match your learning style best support your learning.

3

POINTS TO KEEP IN MIND

In this chapter, the following main points were discussed in detail:

▶ The ability to manage stress and develop good nutritional, exercise, and relaxation habits is essential for optimal learning.

▶ Information is learned more effectively when it is well organized.

▶ Learning occurs when the environment is stable, familiar, and emotionally supportive, as well as challenging.

▶ Learning styles include auditory, visual, tactile, and kinesthetic.

▶ Learning models include Kolb's Learning Style Model, Herrmann Brain Dominance Instrument, and the Felder-Silverman model. The Myer-Briggs Type Indicator, although not a learning model per se, can provide information on how you interact with your environment to facilitate learning.

▶ Active learning requires student involvement in activities such as solving problems, answering questions, formulating questions, discussing, debating, and brainstorming.

▶ Teamwork is a requirement of both academic and professional environments.

▶ Students who excel academically have typically developed skills in efficiently taking notes, completing reading assignments, studying, and taking exams.

▶ How one prepares for an exam is partly dependent upon if the exam is to be objective or essay type.

▶ Hybrid courses combine both online and classroom learning.

LEARNING OBJECTIVES REVISITED

Review the learning objectives for this chapter and rate your level of achievement for each objective using the rating scale provided. For each objective on which you do not rate yourself as a 3, outline a plan of action that you will take to fully achieve the objective. Include a time frame for this plan.

1 = did not successfully achieve objective

2 = understand what is needed, but need more study or practice

3 = achieved learning objective thoroughly

	1	2	3
Define *active learning* and *teamwork*.	☐	☐	☐
Explain how the functions of the brain have an impact on one's learning experience.	☐	☐	☐
Discuss the various learning style models.	☐	☐	☐
Describe an effective study environment.	☐	☐	☐
Explain how to improve reading skills.	☐	☐	☐
Discuss methods to minimize test anxieties.	☐	☐	☐
Explain the steps one can utilize to curb nerves while taking an exam.	☐	☐	☐
Discuss methods used for effective note taking.	☐	☐	☐
Explain the importance of determining one's preferred learning style.	☐	☐	☐
Explain the characteristics of a cohesive team.	☐	☐	☐
Discuss how to minimize math anxieties.	☐	☐	☐
Explain the difference between preparing for an objective exam versus an essay exam.	☐	☐	☐
Explain the basic principles of mnemonics.	☐	☐	☐
Describe a hybrid course.	☐	☐	☐

Steps to Achieve Unmet Objectives

Steps	Due Date
1. _____	_____
2. _____	_____
3. _____	_____
4. _____	_____

SUGGESTED ITEMS FOR LEARNING PORTFOLIO

▶ Learning Models
▶ Memory Techniques

REFERENCES

American Heritage Dictionary of the English Language (4th ed.). (2000). Available at: http://www.bartleby.com/61/

Felder, R. M., & Brent, R. (2003). Learning by doing [Electronic version]. *Chemical Engineering Education, 37*(4), 282–283. Retrieved September 26, 2005, from http://www.ncsu.edu/felder-public/Columns/Active.pdf

Fryer, W. A. (2001–2002). Integrating technology in the classroom: Online courseware options [Electronic version]. (Republished from *TechEdge,* 2001–2002.) Retrieved February 28, 2005, from http://www.wtvi.com/teks/01_02_articles/onlinecourseware.html

Garnham, C., & Kaleta, R. (2002, March). Introduction to hybrid courses [Electronic version]. *Teaching with Technology Today 8*(6). Retrieved February 28, 2005, from http://www.uwsa.edu/ttt/articles/garnham.htm

Maine Support Network. (1997). Understanding a brain-based approach to learning and teaching [Electronic version]. (Adapted from Caine, R. N., & Caine, G., 1990, Understanding a brain-based approach to learning and teaching, *Educational Leadership 48*(2), 66–70.) Retrieved February 28, 2005, from http://www.mainesupportnetwork.org/handouts/html/Approach.htm (Original work published in 1990)

Middlebury College, Office of Learning Resources. (n.d.) *Study skills.* Retrieved September 28, 2005, from http://www.middlebury.edu/academics/tools/olr/study_skills/

NDT Resource Center, Iowa State University. (2001). Teamwork in the classroom [Electronic version]. Retrieved March 1, 2005, from http://www.ndt-ed.org/TeachingResources/ClassroomTips/Teamwork.htm

Pelley, J. W. (2002). The success types learning style type indicator: Introduction to your psychological type [Electronic version]. Texas Tech University Health Sciences Center. Retrieved February 28, 2005, from http://www.ttuhsc.edu/SOM/Success/LSTIntro.htm (Original work published in 1998)

Pucel, D. J., & Fruehling, R. T. (1997). *Working in Teams: Interaction and Communication*. St. Paul, MN: Paradigm Publishing Inc.

Saint Louis University, Department of Mathematics and Computer Science. (1993). Success in mathematics [Electronic version]. Retrieved September 27, 2005, from http://euler.slu.edu/Dept/ Successinmath.html

3

CHAPTER OUTLINE

Critical and Creative Thinking

Problem Solving

Decision Making

Using Professional Resources

4 Critical Thinking and Problem Solving

LEARNING OBJECTIVES

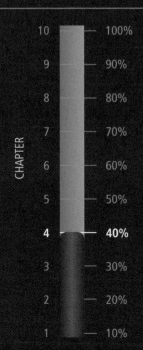

By the end of this chapter, you will achieve the following objectives:

▶ Describe the differences between critical and creative thinking and be able to explain when to use each.

▶ Explain the steps of critical thinking and describe common thinking errors.

▶ Describe the steps of problem solving and apply them to a real-life situation.

▶ Describe the steps of decision making and apply them to a real-life situation.

▶ Explain the importance of using statistics appropriately.

▶ Apply basic concepts of using statistics to critical thinking activities.

TOPIC SCENARIO

Todd Whitmore is employed by a medium-size organization and works in the Research and Development Department. Todd is prompt, has minimal absences, abides by company policy, and follows directions for his assignments accurately. Considering these elements, one might say Todd is a model employee.

Todd, however, is experiencing frustrations. He has worked with this company for over four years and believes that he is ready to be promoted to a more responsible position within the department. He has applied for several positions within the department and has been declined a promotion each time.

Todd recently approached his supervisor to discuss the issue and his frustrations. His supervisor, although supportive, told Todd that even though Todd was a good employee, he needs to develop his critical thinking skills and logical thought processes in order to achieve a promotion. Todd's supervisor gave Todd examples of scenarios where Todd had contributed to problem-solving processes but had not taken into consideration all relevant factors, resulting in an incomplete solution and an inappropriate decision for the department. The supervisor also revealed that Todd needed to be more creative in order to move ahead as a contributor in the department and the company.

Todd's supervisor was supportive of Todd's efforts and desire to expand his responsibilities and skills within the Research and Development Department. Todd and his supervisor proceeded to set goals and devise strategies to help Todd develop his critical and creative thinking abilities. In relation to this scenario, consider the following questions:

▶ What did Todd's supervisor mean by "critical thinking skills" and "logical thought processes"?

▶ What is the difference between critical and creative thinking?

▶ What are some critical thinking processes that Todd might have been lacking?

▶ How do critical thinking skills contribute to effective problem solving and decision making?

▶ What are some methods that Todd might use to develop his critical thinking skills?

▶ What are some methods that Todd might use to develop his creative thinking?

CRITICAL AND CREATIVE THINKING

Critical and creative thinking go hand in hand but are two different processes. Critical thinking is the ability to effectively analyze and use information. Creative thinking is the skill of applying acceptable standards and procedures in an innovative and effective manner. This is sometimes referred to as "thinking out of the box."

CRITICAL THINKING

Critical thinking is a process in which you consider information in a methodical and disciplined manner. Developing your critical thinking skills will benefit you in the classroom as well as in your career by strengthening your ability to present ideas and conclusions supported by accurate data. Critical thinking is also known as logical thinking or analytical thinking.

Critical thinking entails systematic thinking and requires conceptualization, the ability to logically analyze information from multiple perspectives, and the ability to synthesize a conclusion from your analysis. For critical thinking to be useful, you must be able to apply your conclusions to daily activities.

Critical Thinking Processes

Precise thinking skills are necessary in order to think critically. Understanding these skills can help you keep them in your awareness and apply them to your thought processes. Asking yourself questions during the critical thinking process will help you identify important elements to consider. The questions suggested below are based on recommendations from the Foundation for Critical Thinking ("The critical mind is a questioning mind," 2004).

▶ What is my purpose? What am I trying to accomplish?

▶ What question do I need to answer to achieve my goal or purpose?

▶ What information do I need to answer the question?

▶ Is my information from verifiable and reliable sources?

▶ Am I using sound and logical reasoning to make sense of my information and reach a sound conclusion?

▶ Are there alternative perspectives that should be considered?

▶ What conclusions can I make from my information?

▶ Are my conclusions unbiased and logical based on reliable information?

? CRITICAL THINKING QUESTIONS

4–1. How do you define *critical thinking*?

4–2. What are the processes of critical thinking?

▶ REFLECTION QUESTION

• How do you use critical thinking in your daily life? in school?

4

© BananaStock Ltd.

Critical thinking is an important component of successfully completing assignments and includes skills such as conceptualization and analysis of ideas.

The following suggestions are actions you can take to develop critical thinking skills.

Remaining Objective

Personal opinions and values are important but should not be a part of professional decisions. Critical thinking requires the setting aside of personal opinion and judgments. It requires you to evaluate information on the basis of its merits related to the issue at hand and to use valid facts in the process.

Dialectical Thinking

Dialectical thinking is the ability to consider more than one viewpoint or perspective at a time. It is an important part of critical thinking, as it allows you to take into account all aspects of a problem or question. Considering multiple perspectives of an issue helps you to understand the issue in greater depth, which in turn provides the opportunity for more accurate analysis and a more effective presentation of your information.

Breadth and Depth of Thinking

Breadth of thought refers to taking multiple points of view into consideration and is related to dialectical thinking. Consciously consider multiple perspectives that may be related to your subject.

On the other hand, *depth of thought* refers to the level of detail that you consider related to your topic. Determine the amount of detail that you need and present enough information to logically support your point without overwhelming your audience.

Multiple Causality

It is important to recognize that there are usually several causes for any given event. A situation may appear to be a consequence of an action or event, but circumstances are rarely (if ever) products of direct cause and effect. Thinking critically requires consideration of all events and conditions that contribute to a situation.

The Situation and the Context

No two situations are exactly alike. Considering information critically requires taking into account the circumstances, environment, and the individuals who are involved. Each of these individual factors contributes to the uniqueness of each situation, making a customized approach necessary for effective thinking.

On the other hand, past situations that are similar to present circumstances can give you ideas for addressing current issues. Think about past experiences that might lend insight into current thinking. Effective critical thinking requires considering both the differences and similarities of past and current situations.

Using Metacognition

Metacognition is consciously monitoring your thought processes to understand how you are thinking. Researchers Christine Frank and Lynn Davie (2001) emphasize the importance of metacognition in developing critical thinking skills. Pay attention to how you think and the elements of critical thinking that you use. Reflection is the process of thinking back over the way you reached your conclusion and can provide insight into the way that you think. Reflection allows us to understand our assumptions, become more aware, and become conscious of alternatives (Stein, 2000).

---

success steps

ASSESSING YOUR THINKING

1. Know and clearly explain what your reasoning is supposed to achieve.

2. Identify your assumptions, make sure they are valid, and understand how they are influencing your thought process.

3. Identify your point of view and contrast it with others' viewpoints. Understand the strong and weak points of both.

4. Support points of view with quantifiable data.

5. Explain relationships and concepts clearly.

6. Make sure that the points you make are consistent and don't contradict one another.

7. Make sure that the conclusions that you draw are consistent with the concepts and points that you have stated.

These steps are adapted from Paul and Elder (1996).

Obstacles to Critical Thinking

Obstacles to critical thinking occur when information that you have available is considered inaccurately, incompletely, or both. Errors of this nature can result in ineffective decisions and information that is presented in an illogical manner. Developing the habit of making the following considerations will contribute to more effective critical thinking.

Assumption versus Fact

Critical thinking requires you to use solid facts and evidence in your analysis of information. An argument or conclusion loses its credibility

4

when personal biases or assumptions are used as facts supporting a decision or argument. Errors in critical thinking and in subsequent decisions are more likely to occur when assumptions are used in place of verifiable facts.

Thinking Superficially

Superficial thinking means considering only the very obvious or superficial facts and aspects of an issue. Thinking in depth requires identifying related information, considering the context of the issue, and understanding the relationships of all factors. Discussing, writing, diagramming, and reading are methods for delving into an issue in greater depth.

Jumping to Conclusions

Another error in thinking and one that can significantly interfere with effective critical thinking is determining a conclusion before all relevant data is received. If all important facts are not available, it is difficult (if not impossible) to draw a logical conclusion. One element that can contribute to the tendency to jump to conclusions is an emotional reaction to information or circumstances. It is normal and expected to have emotional responses to certain issues that you encounter. However, emotional reactions must be tempered with an objective and rational consideration of the facts in order to think effectively and reach reasonable conclusions.

All-or-None Thinking

All-or none-thinking occurs when one believes that because something happens in a certain way one time, all future events will occur in the same manner. Another aspect of all-or-none thinking is the conviction that because one believes in a certain way, that way of thinking is the only way to think and is always true. All-or-none thinking is believing that there is one universal way to think about something and to apply information. Effective critical thinking requires flexibility, recognizing that there is usually more than one way to do or think about something.

Cause and Effect

Multiplicity, or the idea that events usually have more than one cause, was discussed earlier in this chapter. The related error in critical thinking occurs when an event is viewed as a direct result of another event or situation. It is generally more productive to think in terms of correlated events, or circumstances that are related to a result. Considering one event or circumstance to be the cause of a situation or issue usually limits other aspects of critical thinking, because it limits your perspective. To be credible, you must be able to explain the relationship between the cause and the outcome. Figure 4–1 shows the process of critical thinking.

DIAGRAM OF THE CRITICAL THINKING PROCESS

Define the purpose for your reasoning. $\longrightarrow$ Identify your assumptions. $\longrightarrow$ Identify your point of view and compare it to others' viewpoints. $\longrightarrow$ Clarify and state your point of view and support it with quantifiable data. $\longrightarrow$ Draw and state conclusions.

Ask these questions:	Ask these questions:	Ask these questions:	Ask these questions:
▶ Are you remaining objective? ▶ Are your assumptions valid and relevant? ▶ How are your assumptions affecting your thinking?	▶ What are the strong and weak points of each viewpoint? ▶ Do you need to consider another point of view and possibly incorporate it into your thinking? ▶ Have you considered multiple causes?	▶ Are the relationships clear and logical? ▶ Are the concepts clearly articulated? ▶ Are there any contradictions?	▶ Are your conclusions consistent with the concepts you have presented?

Thinking critically means systematically sorting and analyzing information. Critical thinking is an important skill to develop for school and professional activities. Following the steps outlined here can support you in developing this skill.

Adapted from Paul and Elder (1996).

success steps

STEPS FOR CRITICAL THINKING

1. Differentiate facts from assumptions.
2. Consider issues in depth.
3. Consider all important facts and perspectives before reaching a conclusion.
4. Avoid all-or-none thinking. Expect some ambiguity.
5. Recognize that events usually have multiple causes.

apply it

Problem-Solving Techniques

GOAL: To learn and apply strategies to be used in the problem-solving process.

STEP 1: Conduct an Internet search using "idea mapping," "concept mapping," and "visual learning methods" as your search terms.

continued

continued

STEP 2: Review the results of your searches and select a method that you believe will be effective for you.

STEP 3: Use the method to approach a problem or to arrive at a creative solution.

STEP 4: Reflect on your outcome and compare the results to other problem-solving techniques you have used. Write a brief reflection to include in your Learning Portfolio.

apply it

Critical Thinking Journal

GOAL: *To increase your awareness of your thought processes and to develop your critical thinking skills.*

STEP 1: Understand the elements of critical thinking. You may discover variations on these themes as you complete this activity.

STEP 2: Consciously use these elements in two ways: (1) Analyze information or a problem in your usual manner and reflect on the process to determine which elements you used, and (2) think of each element and apply it to a problem or information that you are analyzing. You may wish to try the first approach followed by the second for the same problem and compare the processes.

STEP 3: Review your critical thinking process. Evaluate what you have learned and think about how you might apply your findings in the future.

STEP 4: Record your thinking process and your observations about your thinking process. Compile your observations into a critical thinking journal. Review your progress regularly.

CREATIVE THINKING

Creative thinking is the ability to sort out problems, identify pressing issues, and arrive at effective solutions. Scott Isaksen and Donald Treffinger (1985, p. 13) define the purpose of creativity as follows:

- To encourage the identification of possibilities
- To think in new and varied ways

> To consider different points of view

> To think of new approaches and strategies

> To generate and encourage the use of new ideas

While critical thinking involves the systematic analysis of information and arriving at logical conclusions based on fact and circumstances, creative thinking is the ability to apply those conclusions in unique ways to meet goals. Creative thinking may also be a part of critical thinking, in that the critical thinking process may require innovative approaches to finding and interpreting information. You will also find that critical thinking has a place in the creative thinking process. There is certainly overlap between the two types of thinking, although you are likely to use each for specific purposes.

Creative thinking can benefit your problem-solving efforts in personal and professional circumstances. The ability to effectively solve problems and manage others in the problem-solving process is a skill that is highly valued by employers and is valued in a world where rapid change occurs as a result of advancing technology and a growing knowledge base.

An important element to keep in mind about creative thinking is that it is not a license to do whatever you want. Effective creative thinking requires the consideration of professional, legal, and ethical boundaries and the development of innovative solutions within acceptable limits.

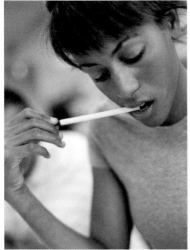

Creative thinking requires reflection to identify problems, generate ideas, and analyze possible solutions.

PROBLEM SOLVING

Isaksen and Treffinger (1985) suggest clearly defined steps to take in the creative problem-solving process. By consciously completing each step, you may be more focused and able to arrive at creative solutions more effectively. Isaksen and Treffinger's creative problem-solving steps are summarized as follows.

MESS FINDING

Mess finding refers to the process of determining an area that might benefit from creative problem solving. Your "mess" might be obvious to you, or you may need to prioritize areas to which you would like to direct your problem-solving efforts.

DATA FINDING

In the *data finding* stage you collect information that will help you begin the problem-solving process. Data can consist of your knowledge, information from other sources, opinions of people whose input you value, and any other facts and figures that are useful to you. You should also record any questions, concerns, or feelings that you have about your "mess." The purpose of this step is to sort out and assess where you stand in the problem-solving process.

PROBLEM FINDING

During this step, you review the information that you have collected and determine if you have accurately pinpointed the problem. Once all of the data has been reviewed, you may find that there are several issues within your "mess" to consider. For example, there may be smaller concerns leading up to the larger problem that will need to be addressed in order of importance. The *problem finding* step is where you clarify and prioritize the most pressing issues.

IDEA FINDING

Idea finding is similar to the brainstorming process that occurs within a group. During this step, you identify as many ideas and approaches to your problem as possible. As you identify ideas, take the same approach as in a brainstorming session. Do not censor or negate any idea. Record all thoughts that come to mind, even if they seem outlandish or impossible. They may be springboards to other ideas. Keep in mind that the more ideas you can generate, the more likely your chance of finding a workable solution. Consider completing this step in several sessions, as you are likely to develop additional ideas over time. Isaksen and Treffinger (1985, p. 18) suggest letting ideas "simmer" to allow new perspectives to come to mind and new ideas to develop. Jot down ideas as they come up so that you don't forget them.

When you are confident that you have accumulated a sufficient number of ideas, begin to sort them by combining similar ideas, determining feasibility, and discarding those that are not practical.

SOLUTION FINDING

In the *solution finding* step you determine the merit of your ideas based on standards and criteria that you have set. Assess the advantages and disadvantages of each idea based on your criteria and decide which ideas have the most potential as a solution for your problem. During this step of the process, you may find it helpful to make a list comparing pros and cons.

ACCEPTANCE FINDING

Acceptance finding is the stage where you put your solution into action. You will consider the strengths of your ideas and avenues to pursue them, as well as anticipate barriers and obstacles that you might encounter. At this stage, some individuals and organizations conduct a SWOT analysis. SWOT stands for

▶ **s**trengths (the strong points of your solution),

▶ **w**eaknesses (components of your solution or skills that you need to develop),

▶ **o**pportunities (possibilities to promote your solution or idea), and

▶ **t**hreats (elements in the environment that may impede your success).

Identifying each of these components reveals the strategies necessary to maximize your chances of success.

The Creative Thinking Process

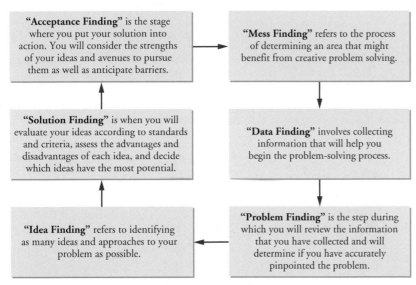

"Acceptance Finding" is the stage where you put your solution into action. You will consider the strengths of your ideas and avenues to pursue them as well as anticipate barriers.

"Mess Finding" refers to the process of determining an area that might benefit from creative problem solving.

"Solution Finding" is when you will evaluate your ideas according to standards and criteria, assess the advantages and disadvantages of each idea, and decide which ideas have the most potential.

"Data Finding" involves collecting information that will help you begin the problem-solving process.

"Idea Finding" refers to identifying as many ideas and approaches to your problem as possible.

"Problem Finding" is the step during which you will review the information that you have collected and will determine if you have accurately pinpointed the problem.

Like critical thinking, creative thinking is a process of steps and consciously considering your options.

Adapted from Isaksen & Treffinger (1985).

success steps

DEVELOPING CREATIVE THINKING SKILLS

1. Carry a small notebook or pad of paper with you and jot down ideas as you think of them.

2. Give ideas time to "brew," as this helps them to develop.

3. Consider *all* ideas, even if they seem outlandish at first.

4. Use creative learning tools, such as idea mapping, to analyze your ideas.

5. Consciously reflect on your thought processes.

4

apply it

Creative Problem Solving

GOAL: *To apply the steps of creative problem solving as defined by Isaksen and Treffinger.*

STEP 1: Identify a topic or issue for which you would like to brainstorm creative options.

STEP 2: Using several sheets of paper, write each one of Isaksen and Treffinger's creative problem-solving steps (mess finding, etc.) at the top of each.

STEP 3: As you complete each step of the problem-solving process, record your thoughts and ideas on the appropriate sheet.

STEP 4: Review each step to understand how you arrived at your solution. Be sure to evaluate your solution for effectiveness. If necessary, review the steps of the process to determine how you might improve the process next time.

apply it

Creative Thinking on the Web

GOAL: *To explore ideas and resources for developing creative thinking and lateral logic and to apply principles of creative problem solving.*

STEP 1: Conduct an Internet search using the search terms "creative thinking," "creative problem solving," and "lateral logic." Look for strategies for creative problem solving that provide steps that you can apply to a real-life issue. Print the articles and strategies that you find most interesting.

STEP 2: Select one of the approaches you find for creative problem solving and familiarize yourself with its principles. You may wish to do further research to learn more about the strategy that you select.

STEP 3: Apply the strategy to a problem that you are currently trying to solve. Follow through on each of the recommended steps and keep a written journal of your progress and findings.

apply it

Group Brainstorming and Problem Solving

GOAL: To gain experience in the brainstorming process and to apply brainstorming to the problem-solving process.

STEP 1: Assemble a group of people who are working to develop a solution to a common problem. This might be related to a school assignment or a project outside of school.

STEP 2: Ensure that all group members understand the ground rules of brainstorming, which are summarized here:

- Consider all ideas for all of the stages of creative problem solving. For example, in the problem finding stage, collect as many ideas as possible regarding what the actual problem is. During idea finding, collect as many ideas as possible for addressing the problem. You may already have identified your "mess" or the issue that you are addressing. If not, you can also implement group brainstorming for mess finding.

- Do not pass judgment on any ideas at this stage of brainstorming.

- Write all ideas on a whiteboard or flip chart. Complete this process for each step of the problem-solving process.

STEP 3: Use brainstorming guidelines to implement the stages of mess finding, problem finding, idea finding, and solution finding.

STEP 4: Following each of the stages of problem solving from Step 3, analyze the ideas that have been generated. Combine similar ideas, sequence suggestions, and organize your information. During this process, you will condense your many ideas into smaller, workable chunks. Distill your many ideas into a workable plan for each step of the problem-solving process.

STEP 5: Implement a SWOT analysis (if appropriate) to implement your plan. This process will be completed over time and its details will depend on your particular project and environment.

DECISION MAKING

The quality of the decisions you make is directly related to the quality of your thinking. Critical thinking processes are essential to decision making. Creative thinking can be a vital element in developing good alternatives

4

for decisions. Major decisions typically require more attention to critical thinking than smaller, everyday decisions. Understanding how critical and creative thinking influence the decision-making process will support you in making more effective decisions.

apply it

Decision-Making Review

GOAL: To reflect on decision making and identify constructive elements, as well as those that may negatively influence the process.

STEP 1: Identify a decision that you need to make. It can be related to school or can be a decision in your personal life.

STEP 2: Using the elements outlined earlier in this chapter (and listed below), create a hard copy or computer document with the elements listed down the left-hand side.

Elements to Consider in Decision Making

- Assumption versus fact (What verifiable facts do I have?)
- Jumping to conclusions (Do I have all the information that is available to make a good decision?)
- All-or-none thinking (Am I considering that there may be other alternatives and some ambiguous areas, or am I thinking in absolutes?)
- Cause and effect (Am I recognizing that events can have multiple causes or a combination of causes? Am I recognizing that my decision might have multiple effects?)

STEP 3: As you go through your decision-making process (which may extend over a period of days or weeks), make notes about the process. Use the document that you have created as your guide and make your notes in the appropriate areas. Create other categories that you believe would clarify your observations.

STEP 4: Review the outcome of your decision and the information that you have recorded during the decision-making process. What was effective? What was less effective? What might you change in your decision-making strategies?

USING PROFESSIONAL RESOURCES

An important strategy to ensure that you are supporting your thinking, problem solving, and decision making effectively is to use professional literature and resources. All fields have a body of information that is accepted as a professional knowledge base. To be credible, you must be aware of and apply this knowledge base in your professional activities. Before using any statistics, it is important to assess whether your source is reliable. Chapter 8 discusses the credibility of resources and provides guidelines for evaluating credibility.

THE USE OF STATISTICS AND QUANTITATIVE DATA

Statistics and quantitative data (numbers and other "hard" data) can be useful in supporting your thinking and decisions. Statistics are generally viewed as credible supporting evidence to arguments and plans. However, statistics can be misleading and must be used appropriately to be effective. Elements such as the context that the statistic is drawn from, the wording, and other factors influence the trustworthiness of a statistic. The following are some elements to think about when using statistics or other data as part of your reasoning.

Reading Research

When you are reading research in your field, it is important to understand how the research terms and processes are used. Although introductory research is beyond the scope of this text, there are some general points to understand.

In their book on research analysis, Jeffrey Gliner and George Morgan (1997) summarize the following important concepts to consider when using or reading research that uses statistics:

- Statistical analysis is used to show a correlation between events. Statistics do not *prove* cause and effect.

- Correct use of statistics and statistical analysis depends on several factors, including the way in which the study or the presentation of information is designed.

- It is helpful to acquire a basic understanding of quantitative research analyses, for example, *t*-tests and analysis of variance (ANOVA), so that you can better understand how information is being compared and interpreted.

- It is helpful to understand terminology such as *independent variable*, *dependent variable*, and *significance*.

4

The depth to which you need to understand research techniques and strategies will depend on your field. Your specific program curriculum will address research appropriate to your field and education.

Using Statistics Effectively

There may be times when you wish to consider statistics in your critical thinking and decision making. It is important to understand how you are using statistics in order to present your points in a credible and valid manner.

The Online Writing Lab at Purdue University ("Using statistics," n.d.) suggests examining terms such as *average* and *percentage*. It is necessary to know the basis of averages and percentages in order to understand what they mean. For example, if a claim is made that 50% of students have grade point averages above 80%, do you mean 50% of a class, an entire school, or all college students in the country? The numbers are quite different, depending on the basis of the percentage. In addition, "above 80%" is a relatively wide range. What is the percentage really stating? What is the relationship of the statistic to the point you are making?

SOURCES OF PROFESSIONAL RESOURCES

The resources that you have available to you will depend on your field. Generally, the most effective resources are available from publications and documents that are published by professional organizations and academic institutions. Chapter 8 discusses sources of professional literature and information in depth.

CHAPTER SUMMARY

This chapter summarized critical and creative thinking and provided suggestions for using both processes effectively. You learned critical thinking processes and their relationship to decision making, and explored obstacles to critical thinking. You learned an approach to creative thinking and steps that can be used to arrive at solutions to problems you encounter. Finally, you received an overview of the use of statistics and professional data in critical thinking. You are encouraged to expand on this information in a manner appropriate to your field of study.

Critical and creative thinking skills can be applied to your academic and professional development in many ways. In addition to using critical and creative thinking techniques in your studies, consider how they can be applied to your development of the areas covered in *100% Student Success*. For example, concepts of problem solving can be applied to troubleshooting

When giving presentations or using statistics in other classroom projects, be sure to define the context of your statistical terms so that your information is clear and logical.

difficulties with studying or preparing for exams. Decision-making skills can be applied to financial decisions and creative solutions can be found for balancing a busy schedule. You are encouraged to keep critical and creative thinking concepts in mind throughout your work with this text.

POINTS TO KEEP IN MIND

In this chapter, several main points were discussed in detail:

- Critical and creative thinking are separate, yet related, processes.
- Critical thinking is a process in which you consider information in a methodical and disciplined manner.
- Critical thinking involves the use of certain skills such as considering multiple perspectives, understanding multiple causality, conceptualizing, and analyzing data logically.
- Metacognition is the ability to think about and understand your own thinking process and is an important factor in the critical thinking process.
- Errors in thinking, such as jumping to conclusions, using assumptions rather than facts, thinking superficially, engaging in all-or-none thinking, and assuming cause-and-effect relationships, can impede the critical thinking process.
- The purposes of creative thinking include increasing awareness of possibilities, encouraging new ways to think, and considering multiple points of view. Creative thinking techniques help us think in new ways and generate new ideas.
- Effective problem solving and appropriate creative thinking are skills that are highly valued by employers.
- Effective problem-solving skills are imperative in a world where rapid change occurs as a result of advancing technology and a growing knowledge base.
- There are clearly defined steps to take in the creative problem-solving process. By consciously completing each step, you may be more focused and successful in your problem-solving efforts.
- An important strategy to ensure that you are supporting your thinking, problem solving, and decision making effectively is to use professional literature and resources.
- It is important to understand how you are using statistics in order to present your points in a credible and valid manner.

LEARNING OBJECTIVES REVISITED

Review the learning objectives for this chapter and rate your level of achievement for each objective using the rating scale provided. For each objective on which you do not rate yourself as a 3, outline a plan of action that you will take to fully achieve the objective. Include a time frame for this plan.

1 = did not successfully achieve objective

2 = understand what is needed, but need more study or practice

3 = achieved learning objective thoroughly

	1	2	3
Describe the differences between critical and creative thinking and be able to explain when to use each.	☐	☐	☐
Explain the steps of logical thinking and describe common thinking errors.	☐	☐	☐
Describe steps of problem solving and apply them to a real-life situation.	☐	☐	☐
Describe steps of decision making and apply them to a real-life situation.	☐	☐	☐
Explain the importance of using statistics appropriately.	☐	☐	☐
Apply basic concepts of using statistics to critical thinking activities.	☐	☐	☐

Steps to Achieve Unmet Objectives

Steps   Due Date

1. _____   _____

2. _____   _____

3. _____   _____

4. _____   _____

SUGGESTED ITEMS FOR LEARNING PORTFOLIO

▶ Reflection and Critical Thinking Questions: Include your written responses to these questions. Use them to review your development over time.

REFERENCES

The critical mind is a questioning mind: Learning how to ask powerful, probing questions [Electronic version]. (2004). Foundation for Critical Thinking. Retrieved February 16, 2005, from http://www.criticalthinking.org/resources/articles/critical-mind.shtml

Frank, C., & Davie, L. (2001). Creating online communities for critical thinking, reading, and writing. Paper presented at TCC (Teaching in the Community Colleges) 2001 Online Conference. Kapi'olani Community College, The University of Hawaii. Retrieved February 15, 2005, from http://makahiki.Kcc.hawaii.edu/tcc/tcon01/papers/frank.html

Gliner, J. A., & Morgan, G. A. (1997). *Research Design and Analysis in Applied Settings.* Fort Collins, CO: Colorado State University.

Isaksen, S. G., & Treffinger, D. J. (1985). *Creative Problem Solving: The Basic Course.* Buffalo, NY: Bearly Limited.

Paul, R., & Elder, L. (1996, June). The analysis and assessment of thinking (Helping students assess their thinking). Foundation for Critical Thinking. Retrieved February 16, 2005, from http://www.criticalthinking.org/resources/articles/helping-students-assess-their-thinking.shtml

Stein, D. (2000). Teaching critical reflection [Electronic version]. Ohio State University, College of Education, Center on Education and Training for Employment. Retrieved February 16, 2005, from http://www.cete.org/acve/docgen.asp?tbl=mr&ID=98

Using statistics [Electronic version]. (n.d.) Purdue University, Online Writing Lab. Retrieved April 27, 2006, from http://owl.english.purdue.edu/handouts/research/r_stats.html

CHAPTER OUTLINE

5

Legal and Ethical Issues in the Academic Environment

THE BIG PICTURE

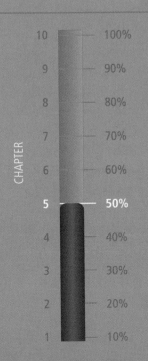

LEARNING OBJECTIVES

By the end of this chapter, you will achieve the following objectives:

▶ Define *academic dishonesty*.

▶ Define *harassment, sexual harassment,* and *discrimination*.

▶ List and discuss the various laws that prohibit discrimination.

▶ Provide examples of legal and ethical issues affecting college students.

▶ Explain the purpose of the Americans with Disabilities Act (ADA) and discuss how this act protects students.

▶ Explain the differences among the Rehabilitation Act of 1973, the Individuals with Disabilities Education Act, and the ADA.

▶ Discuss the obligations that institutions have toward students with disabilities.

▶ Describe the steps involved in reporting sexual harassment.

▶ Discuss ways to avoid the pressure to cheat.

▶ Explain the purpose of Family Educational Rights and Privacy Act (FERPA).

▶ Demonstrate the ability to effectively resolve a conflict.

TOPIC SCENARIO

Finishing college was always Susan McPhee's dream. When she walked across the stage to accept her diploma, all she felt was joy and excitement. She had accomplished her life's dream of having a college education. School had not always been easy and Susan had to overcome many challenges, but in the end she had prevailed. Susan was the first one in her family to obtain a college degree and, consequently, her feelings of pride were even greater. At her first job after college, Susan excelled. She went on to have many successes in her profession. Her last job before retirement was as an entrepreneur and owner of her own business. What makes Susan's story quite unique is that Susan was born blind and as a young girl had been in an accident in which both of her arms were severed. Based on this short description of Susan's life, answer the following questions:

- Over what unique challenges did Susan have to prevail? (In addition to the obvious physical challenges, consider the social and emotional aspects of her situation.)

- What characteristics did Susan need in order to overcome the challenges facing her?

- What laws supported Susan in her effort to complete her education? What recourse did Susan have under these laws in the event of discrimination based on her disability?

- What type of challenges do you think you may have in college and in life that you will need to learn to overcome?

- What characteristics do you have that will help you overcome obstacles? What characteristics do you need to develop?

- What types of accommodations do you suppose Susan's college and employers needed to make in order for her to be successful in college and business?

- How do you think you might react to a classmate who has these disabilities?

- Do you think all disabilities can be overcome? Explain your answer.

LEGAL AND ETHICAL ISSUES: OVERVIEW

It is the responsibility of every college student to know the policies and procedures established by the college they are attending. Students can usually find policies and regulations they should be aware of in the college catalog and/or student handbook. Specific information regarding the history of the college, its mission statement, and its accreditations and affiliations is also generally found in the college catalog. More general information, such as descriptions of school programs, admission requirements, and available financial aid programs, can also be found in the catalog. Students must take responsibility to read and be aware of what is required of and available to them at the college they will be or are attending. "I didn't know" or "no one told me" is not an acceptable excuse for being unaware of expectations and resources.

There are also a variety of legal considerations in the academic environment with which students should be familiar. By understanding these legal matters, students are better protected, more likely to avoid problems, and know the steps to take if a problem occurs. Legal standards having an impact on the academic environment include those that affect policy dealing with sexual harassment, disability, and other types of discrimination.

Some issues in the academic environment are considered to be of both a legal and an ethical nature. For example, confidentiality is an issue that can be viewed from both legal and ethical perspectives. Depending on the situation, it may not be illegal to share information with another person, but the breach may also be considered ethically wrong.

In addition to legal issues, there are ethical principles that must guide behavior in the college environment. Cheating and plagiarizing are actions that have serious ethical (and possibly legal) implications. It is important to not only understand the seriousness of academic dishonesty but also be aware of its consequences.

This chapter will focus on the legal and ethical issues affecting the college environment, how to avoid potential problems, how to document concerns, how and when to report a complaint, and how to effectively address and hopefully resolve the conflict.

Understanding legal issues that affect you as a student can help you avoid difficulties as well as help you understand what steps to take should legal questions arise.

▶ REFLECTION QUESTION

- Have you ever engaged in any behaviors that were legally or ethically questionable? If so, how did you resolve them?

apply it

Ethical Issue Research

GOAL: *To develop a deeper appreciation regarding the ethical issues that students face in the college environment.*

STEP 1: Select one of the references listed in this chapter or find another article or book that discusses various ethical issues that are faced in the college environment.

STEP 2: Write a brief report on what the article or book teaches you.

STEP 3: Prepare a presentation to the class utilizing presentation tools such as PowerPoint.

? CRITICAL THINKING QUESTION

5–1. What other legal and ethical issues can you think of that might be important to consider on a college campus?

LEGAL ISSUES: HARASSMENT AND DISCRIMINATION

There are a variety of legal issues with which students should be familiar. This chapter will focus on legal issues such as sexual harassment and other types of discrimination that can occur on college campuses. In addition to the laws established to protect individuals encountering these issues, schools usually have written policies and procedures to address these situations. Refer to the college handbook and catalog for information on the policies and procedures specific to your school.

Discrimination is defined in civil rights laws as unfavorable or unfair treatment of a person or class of persons in comparison to others who are not members of the protected class, because of race, sex, color, religion, national origin, age, physical/mental disability, or sexual orientation.

The Office for Civil Rights (OCR) in the U.S. Department of Education is charged with enforcing the federal civil rights laws that prohibit discrimination. A variety of laws exist to prohibit discrimination, including:

▶ Title VI of the Civil Rights Act of 1964, which prohibits discrimination due to race, color, or national origin

▶ Title IX of the Education Amendments of 1972, which prohibits sex discrimination

▶ Section 504 of the Rehabilitation Act of 1973, which prohibits discrimination based on an individual's disability

▶ Title II of the Americans with Disabilities Act of 1990, which prohibits disability discrimination by public entities, including educational institutions, and provides for accommodations to be made to facilitate the functioning of people with disabilities (U.S. Department of Education Office for Civil Rights, 2003).

Figure 5–1 summarizes the civil rights laws.

Discrimination can occur in a variety of situations. In 2003, enforcement officers of the OCR received 5,141 discrimination complaints. The OCR (2003, p. 2) breaks down the complaints as follows:

▶ 52% disability

▶ 19% race/national origin

▶ 12% multiple

▶ 7% sex

▶ 9% other

▶ 1% age

SUMMARY OF MAJOR CIVIL RIGHTS LAWS

Law	Provisions
Title VI of the Civil Rights Act of 1964	Prohibits discrimination due to race, color, and national origin
Title IX of the Education Amendments of 1972	Prohibits sex discrimination
Section 504 of the Rehabilitation Act of 1973	Prohibits discrimination based on an individual's disability
Title II of the Americans with Disabilities Act of 1990	Prohibits disability discrimination by public entities, including educational institutions

Understanding civil rights laws will help you understand your rights as well as respect those of others. For more detailed information regarding individual laws, conduct Internet research using the name of the law as your search term.

Adapted from U.S. Department of Education, Office for Civil Rights (2004, p.1).

As the statistics indicate, discrimination can occur for a variety of reasons. Any individual can be the target of discrimination. As a student, it is important to be aware of discrimination and know how to effectively address the situation. Discrimination can occur secondarily to several circumstances common in education environments. Discipline practices, academic grading practices, treatment of pregnant students, admissions practices, and treatment of students with disabilities can all result in students being treated differently in various situations, increasing the possibility of discrimination.

It is important to be informed and knowledgeable about your responsibilities and the college's responsibilities related to discrimination.

SEXUAL HARASSMENT

Awareness of sexual harassment issues on college campuses has increased. In order to address sexual harassment issues, colleges have worked toward having clear definitions of what constitutes sexual harassment and toward creating policies on these issues.

Harassment of any kind should not be tolerated. There are a variety of types of harassment that can occur on a college campus. All types result in an environment that is negative, creates hostility, and undermines productivity.

Sexual harassment occurs when unwelcome attention of a sexual nature occurs between individuals. Sexual harassment may involve two students or can involve an instructor and a student. Society generally thinks of sexual harassment as a male harassing a female. Although this may be the more typical type of harassment, harassment can also involve a female harassing a male, a female harassing a female, or a male harassing a male. In addition, sexual harassment can take several forms:

▶ **Verbal.** Making comments that reflect evaluation and ranking of sexual attributes, inquiring about or suggesting sexual activity, or making unwanted or derogatory comments fall into the category of sexual harassment. Threats or demands to engage in sexual activity to achieve a benefit, obtain or keep a job, or achieve academically are also sexual harassment.

▶ **Visual.** Cartoons, posters, and other visual representations of material of a sexual nature fall into the category of sexual harassment.

▶ **Electronic.** Sexual harassment includes derogatory comments of a sexual nature sent via voice mail, e-mail, or telephone.

▶ **Physical.** Inappropriate physical contact of a sexual nature as well as assault constitute sexual harassment.

▶ **Retaliatory.** Actions in retaliation for having reported harassment fall under the same guidelines as sexual harassment.

At times sexual harassment can occur unintentionally. For example, an individual may make a lewd comment and later realize the inappropriateness of having done so. Due to the harmful effects that sexual harassment can have on individuals, it is critical to be consciously aware of an event or action that may be construed as harassment. If you make a comment that in retrospect seems inappropriate, follow up with the person to ensure that no offense was taken and to rectify any misunderstandings.

Title IX regulations require that all educational institutions that receive federal financial assistance publish and provide a nondiscrimination policy, have a published grievance procedure for dealing with sexual harassment complaints, and designate an individual to oversee Title IX activities and process grievances. The individual designated to coordinate Title IX activities at your school can provide guidelines for documenting grievances, which are likely to vary between schools. In general, documentation should be thorough and clear and include information such as the date, time, and location of the incident, and any witnesses.

REFLECTION QUESTIONS

- Have you ever felt sexually harassed? If so, what was the outcome?
- Can you recall ever sexually harassing somebody unintentionally? Did you take any action to correct your behavior? If not, why? If so, how?

success steps

STEPS FOR REPORTING SEXUAL HARASSMENT

1. Know the individual on your campus who oversees Title IX requirements and activities.

2. Document (a) what happened in as much detail as possible, (b) the location of the incident, (c) the date and time, and (d) any witnesses.

3. Report the incident to your school official immediately.

4. Follow the steps that are recommended by your school's Title IX official.

During any phase of a discrimination incident or its reporting, the student who has experienced the harassment should feel free to ask for help or advice from trusted school advisors, faculty, or other administrative personnel.

DISCRIMINATION AND DISABILITY

The Americans with Disabilities Act (ADA) defines a person with a disability as someone who

- has a physical or mental impairment that substantially limits one or more major life activities including walking, seeing, hearing, speaking, breathing, learning, and working
- has a record of such an impairment
- is regarded as having such an impairment (United States Department of Justice, 2004).

Since schools receive federal funding, they are required to comply with the ADA. General requirements for complying with the ADA state that

- A student with a disability must disclose the disability to the appropriate school personnel and request accommodations.
- The school is required to make accommodations that allow a student to participate in academic and extracurricular programs and activities and complete course requirements. Examples of accommodations include course substitutions, adjustments to academic activities such as note taking (for example, having a note taker for a student who cannot write) and test taking (for example, extra time to complete an exam). Accommodations are specific to the student and will vary according to the needs of the student and the school's situation.

If a student believes that discrimination has occurred, communication with school officials is critical to resolving the issue. Some colleges establish a student legal department to assist students in areas dealing with civil law questions or problems. Many schools also have a department or office, such as Student Services or Student Affairs, that is specifically designated to support students with disabilities and to address any related issues. Check to determine the appropriate office at your school. If a resolution with school officials is not possible, it may be necessary to contact the Office for Civil Rights for further assistance.

If you believe that you have been the target of harassment, it may be helpful to seek the advice and support of a trusted instructor or administrator.

? CRITICAL THINKING QUESTIONS

5–2. What would your reaction be to the following statement made to you after you have told a classmate that his joke was offensive? "It was just a joke. What's the big deal?"

5–3. If an individual came to you and wanted to confide in you about having been sexually harassed, how would you respond? What type of response might be the most helpful?

Equal opportunity and accessibility of campus facilities to students with disabilities is required by federal laws.

5

CONFIDENTIAL INFORMATION

Confidentiality can be both an ethical and a legal issue. Confidentiality must be a primary consideration during verbal communication. Damage that can occur from disclosing information of a confidential nature may be permanent, even though the sharing of information may not have been illegal. Trust is an important component of relationships among students, their teachers, and administrators. If there is reason to believe that confidentiality has been breached, you should raise the issue with the individual involved.

The Family Educational Rights and Privacy Act (FERPA) defines specific guidelines for access to and confidentiality regarding your school records (U.S. Department of Education, n.d.). Laws regarding confidentially issues in the academic setting deal specifically with the student record. Legal information contained in student education records is protected by FERPA. According to FERPA, students over the age of 18 have the right to

- inspect and review their education records

- request that the school correct inaccurate or misleading information that is found in the student record

If the school decides not to change the record, then the student has a right to a formal hearing. If this hearing does not lead to the school amending the record, the student has the right to place a statement in the record indicating his or her viewpoint on the information that is being contested.

FERPA gives schools the right to

- charge a fee for a copy of student records.

- refuse to provide copies to parents and students unless distance is an issue.

- disclose "directory" information without consent. This information includes the student's name, address, telephone number, date and place of birth, honors and awards, and dates of attendance. Schools must inform students of the request for directory information within a time frame that is reasonable, so that the student has a chance to request that the information not be disclosed.

Generally, schools are required to obtain written permission in order to release information from a student's record. FERPA does allow for some instances where permission need not be obtained. The courts may allow advisors, faculty, and administrators to share information on students if there is a "legitimate need to know" as specified by FERPA. Schools are also required to inform students on an annual basis of their rights under FERPA.

apply it

Legal Research

GOAL: *To develop a deeper understanding regarding the legal issues that affect college students.*

STEP 1: From the various laws discussed in this chapter, select one law to research further.

STEP 2: Read everything about the selected law and then write a report to present to the class. Include in the report what was learned regarding the effects of the law for both the school and the student.

STEP 3: Consider placing this Legal Research activity in your Learning Portfolio.

5

ETHICAL ISSUES: ACADEMIC HONESTY

Acting honorably and with integrity are significant universal values. People generally expect and respect truthful and honest interactions and behavior. It is important for students to demonstrate these qualities in all academic activities. The importance of honesty and integrity in both school and the workplace cannot be overstated. Academic dishonesty occurs when a student cheats or engages in plagiarism.

CHEATING

Cheating involves obtaining and/or providing information by deceitful means. Examples of cheating based on those listed in a college honor code (Foothill College, 2005) include the following behaviors:

▶ Copying part or all of another student's test answers or assignment.

▶ Handing in another student's previously completed work as your own.

▶ Resubmitting work that you have written, but used previously in another course. (This is acceptable if doing so is part of the assignment from either course and is stated as such.)

▶ Altering grades in hard copy or electronically.

▶ Using unauthorized equipment such as calculators or unauthorized other aids during an exam.

©Image 100 Ltd.

Academic honesty is an important value critical to the development of sound business ethics.

5

- Seeking information electronically, such as by cell phone or e-mail during an exam.
- Obtaining test material by stealing, electronic pirating, or other methods.

The act of cheating and plagiarizing is harmful to both the college and the student body. Cheating is hurtful in many ways to both the honest and the dishonest student. Honest students become frustrated with the fact that cheating is unfair. The student who cheats fails to learn information that he or she will need in subsequent courses and in the workplace.

Cheating at times goes undetected. In some instances the cheating results in an undeserved grade. If a grading curve is being used in the class, grades received by cheating students can skew the curve, ultimately affecting grades earned by honest students. Students who cheat do not benefit from the education that they are paying for and are jeopardizing their future employment successes because they lack the knowledge needed to perform tasks required by employers. Employers expecting qualified graduates are robbed by cheating students, as is the reputation of the college and future graduates.

Students cheat for a variety of reasons. Penn State University (2000) conducted a survey that analyzed the reasons students cheat and found the following reasons and percentages of students:

- 76% experience pressure for grades
- 46% fear failing family expectations
- 31% say others get away with it
- 22% find instructors too demanding
- 19% claim instructors don't prevent cheating
- 18% don't feel it's wrong
- 11% experience a challenge to do so
- 8% only face minor penalties
- 6% are confused about cheating
- 5% feel it's OK at Penn State University to cheat

As indicated, the pressure to get good grades and the pressure to meet family expectations are the top two reasons why students cheat. Although these pressures do exist, it is important for students to weigh these pressures against the consequences of cheating. Consequences of cheating can include:

- Receiving an F for the work
- Receiving a lower course grade or an F
- Failing a class that is required for graduation

▶ Being suspended or dismissed from school

▶ Damaging your reputation with other classmates, instructors, and family members

In many cases, students' own personal beliefs deter them from cheating. The same Penn State survey yielded the following results regarding factors that keep students from cheating:

▶ Personal beliefs (74%)

▶ Chances of getting caught (66%)

▶ Potential penalties (52%)

▶ Academic integrity expectations (29%)

▶ Respect for instructors (25%)

As a college student, it is important to appreciate the importance of maintaining your personal integrity and to understand the consequences of your actions and how they affect others. Students who uphold academic integrity will more likely follow the standards and ethics that are required later in their professions. For some students, the pressure to cheat at some point in the college experience may be high. If you experience this temptation, rather than cheat, stop to determine why the pressure to act dishonestly exists. Instead of cheating, try implementing one of the following strategies based on Kibler and Vannoy Kibler (1998):

▶ **Use time management techniques.** Develop study habits that give you ample time to learn course material.

▶ **Develop your classroom and study skills.** Develop your listening, note-taking, and reading skills. Compare your notes with classmates' and determine what you missed and how you might improve. If in doubt, ask the instructor. Develop a study area that is conducive to studying and that supports your efforts. Clarify information with the instructor as needed. Understand your learning style in order to increase the effectiveness of your studying; use a study method that best supports your style.

▶ **Seek assistance when needed.** If information is difficult or unclear, ask questions of the instructor. Use the learning resource center on campus or obtain a tutor. Get assistance promptly to avoid feeling overwhelmed.

▶ **Individualize your learning.** Recognize your individual learning needs and seek additional activities that will support you in the learning process.

▶ **Maintain your integrity.** Refuse to be a part of dishonest actions.

5

5

STEPS TO AVOID THE TEMPTATION TO CHEAT

1. Use time management techniques.
2. Develop your classroom and study skills.
3. Seek assistance when needed.
4. Individualize your learning.
5. Maintain your integrity.

PLAGIARISM

Plagiarism is using another person's work as your own without giving appropriate credit to the author or source in a citation or reference. Note that plagiarism can apply to the written word, illustrations and other art, music, and electronic media. The following examples are based on those found in the Foothill College honor code and *Keys for Writers* by Ann Raimes (1996). Plagiarism is

- using another author's information and stating that you wrote or created it
- not properly acknowledging a direct quotation
- summarizing facts or opinions from sources without stating exactly where they come from
- exceeding the permissible limit of information directly quoted from another source
- buying, finding, or receiving a paper and turning it in as your own work

Plagiarism can be avoided by implementing specific steps. Knowing what constitutes plagiarism is significant. In addition, consider the following steps:

- **Manage your time.** Plan your studying and assignments so that you have time to plan, research, and write your work effectively. Leave time to read and write with careful attention to citing sources and representing other authors' works in an acceptable manner.
- **Know what constitutes plagiarism.** Copying verbatim, using someone else's ideas or thoughts without giving proper credit, and claiming another's work as your own are all clear examples of plagiarism. Paraphrasing and changing the order of words is also considered plagiarism.

▶ **Read and rewrite.** An effective way to avoid plagiarizing is to read the original source, put it away, and complete your writing based on your reading. When your writing is complete, return to the original work and check your facts for accuracy. Cite references appropriately.

▶ **Apply the information.** Discuss the information you are using in the context of your assignment. Expand on ideas. Apply the information in a unique way to the topic at hand. Refer to the original thought or fact, but apply it creatively to your project using your own original ideas.

▶ **Cite your sources appropriately.** Sources should be referenced in the text as well as in the reference list. There are several acceptable styles of source citation and reference, and you should follow the style prescribed by your instructor.

▶ **Use direct quotes correctly.** Direct quotes can be used, but they must be indicated as such (usually in quotation marks or set apart from the main text) and referenced appropriately according to the style you are using. Check your style guide for length limitations on direct quotes, as exceeding stated limits can constitute plagiarism.

success steps

STEPS FOR AVOIDING PLAGIARISM

1. Manage your time.
2. Know what constitutes plagiarism.
3. Read and rewrite.
4. Apply the information.
5. Cite your sources appropriately.
6. Use direct quotes correctly.

In addition to your own responsibility for being honest, it is important to participate in helping to make your learning environment one of high integrity. Honest students need to report any possibly cheating and plagiarism that may be occurring. Personally confronting a classmate may or may not be an option, but reporting the episode is critical so that the situation can be properly addressed.

5

©Image 100 Ltd.

Learning to resolve conflicts calmly, respectfully, and logically with concern for everyone's welfare is an important professional skill.

CONFLICT RESOLUTION

Conflict resolution is a useful skill for addressing a variety of the topics that have been covered in this chapter. Having to confront an individual who is making lewd comments, demonstrating discriminatory behavior, or asking to plagiarize your work can be quite challenging. Learning how to appropriately confront issues and resolve them effectively is a skill that can be utilized in both the academic and professional settings.

Conflict is inevitable and will occur throughout life. For some, conflict resolution is a skill that develops naturally. For others, confronting an issue and resolving it can be difficult. Conflict resolution should be thought of as a series of positive steps taken toward understanding another individual and the situation at hand.

If conflict arises, consider the following steps:

Step 1. Don't simply react emotionally to the situation. Thoughtfully plan the best approach to the situation. Determine mutually what both parties hope to achieve by resolving the conflict.

Step 2. Approach the conflict with an attitude of trying to understand the other person, his or her perspective, and the situation.

Step 3. Assume that the person you are approaching has good intentions. Avoid jumping to conclusions. Ask questions to clarify the meaning of the person's words and his or her intentions.

Step 4. Use voice tones that are neither condoning nor condemning. Avoid raising your voice. Keep an open mind and be accepting of other ideas and perspectives.

Step 5. Be clear with the individual about your concerns. Share your thoughts as clearly and concisely as possible.

Step 6. Use "I" statements rather than "you" statements when expressing your thoughts. For example, state "I feel really upset" or "I am not sure I understand what to do." Pointing the finger by saying "you did this" and "you made me feel" may sound accusatory and is unlikely to facilitate effective communication.

Step 7. Find common ground on which you can agree.

Step 8. Accept that a difference of opinion can exist. Agree to disagree, but remain respectful of each other.

Step 9. If you are in the wrong, acknowledge this. Seek to implement changes that will be beneficial to all concerned.

Step 10. Make necessary changes. Learn from the conflict resolution process.

success steps

RESOLVING CONFLICT

1. Remain objective and keep emotions under control.
2. Try to understand the other person's perspective.
3. Assume the other party has good intentions.
4. Speak in a conversational tone of voice.
5. State your concerns clearly and directly.
6. Use "I" statements rather than "you" statements.
7. Find common ground on which you both agree.
8. Respect differences.
9. If you are wrong, acknowledge it.
10. Make necessary changes.

These steps can also be used when questioning a professor about grades. Often the conflict or misunderstanding about a grade or a situation in class can be resolved by using the steps as outlined. Depending on the situation, implementing these steps may be difficult. Although it may be difficult, the instructor should be approached first in an attempt to resolve the issue. If this is unsuccessful, then talking to a department chair, the assistant dean, or your advisor may be the next option. It is important to understand that instructors want to hear about students' concerns. Sometimes students are upset or unhappy, but the instructor is unaware of the situation. As much as possible, communicate directly with each instructor. Remember that approaching the individual with whom you have an issue is the preferred method of handling conflict before going to another party. Building relationships and trust is important.

Conflict resolution can often be achieved by approaching the issue directly and openly and speaking with the individual(s) involved. Remember the importance of establishing and maintaining trust in the conflict resolution process.

apply it

Conflict Resolution

GOAL: To help develop skills in conflict resolution through role playing.

Prior to this activity the instructor should prepare a variety of scenarios in which conflict arises and resolution is achieved. Alternatively, pairs of students may write scenarios to be distributed to the class. Students may write a scenario that they personally experienced or describe a situation that they believe would be difficult for them to address.

continued

continued

STEP 1: Divide the class into the appropriate numbers of individuals for each scenario.

STEP 2: Hand out a scenario to each group. (If students have written the scenarios, they should not receive their own).

STEP 3: Each group is to practice role playing the scenario. Once the scenarios have been successfully acted out, have group members switch roles and replay the scenario.

STEP 4: Regroup as a class and discuss what was learned in the activity. What was difficult about resolving the conflict? What was learned through trying to resolve the conflict? What might have been improved during the conflict resolution?

CHAPTER SUMMARY

This chapter addressed issues related to legal and ethical concerns in the academic setting. You learned about various laws that affect you as a student, as well as your responsibilities for your conduct and honest behavior. Take notice of how methods of time management, note taking, and other techniques that have been discussed so far in *100% Student Success* can be used to contribute to other considerations such as academic honesty. In addition, topics such as understanding plagiarism will be critical to becoming information literate, discussed in Chapter 8. The communication skills reviewed in Chapter 9 will be important to the development of conflict resolution skills.

POINTS TO KEEP IN MIND

In this chapter, a variety of main points were discussed in detail:

- Legal issues common in the academic environment include those dealing with sexual harassment and other various types of discrimination.
- Sexual harassment can be defined as unwanted attention of a sexual nature.
- Any type of harassment creates a hostile or intimidating environment.
- Title IX regulations require that all education institutions have a published grievance procedure that is adequate for dealing with sexual harassment complaints.

▶ Discrimination is defined in civil rights laws as unfavorable or unfair treatment of a person or class of persons in comparison to others who are not members of the protected class because of race, sex, color, religion, national origin, age, physical/mental disability, and sexual orientation.

▶ Title IX of the Education Amendments of 1972 prohibits sex discrimination.

▶ Section 504 of the Rehabilitation Act of 1973 prohibits discrimination based on an individual's disability.

▶ Title II of the Americans with Disabilities Act of 1990 prohibits disability discrimination by public entities, including educational institutions.

▶ Legal information contained in student education records is protected by the Family Educational Rights and Privacy Act (FERPA).

▶ Generally, schools are required to obtain written permission in order to release information from a student's education record.

▶ Schools are required to inform students on an annual basis of the rights students have through FERPA.

▶ Academic dishonesty occurs when a student cheats or engages in plagiarism.

▶ The act of cheating and plagiarizing is harmful to the college, the student body, employers, and future graduates.

▶ Conflict resolution should be thought of as a series of positive steps taken toward understanding another individual.

LEARNING OBJECTIVES REVISITED

Review the learning objectives for this chapter and rate your level of achievement for each objective using the rating scale provided. For each objective on which you do not rate yourself as a 3, outline a plan of action that you will take to fully achieve the objective. Include a time frame for this plan.

1 = did not successfully achieve objective

2 = understand what is needed, but need more study or practice

3 = achieved learning objective thoroughly

	1	2	3
Define *academic dishonesty*.	☐	☐	☐
Define *harassment, sexual harassment,* and *discrimination.*	☐	☐	☐
List and discuss the various laws that prohibit discrimination.	☐	☐	☐
Provide examples of legal and ethical issues affecting college students.	☐	☐	☐
Explain the purpose of the Americans with Disabilities Act (ADA) and discuss how this Act protects students.	☐	☐	☐
Explain the differences among the Rehabilitation Act of 1973, the Individuals with Disabilities Education Act, and the ADA.	☐	☐	☐
Discuss the obligations that institutions have toward students with disabilities.	☐	☐	☐
Describe the steps involved in reporting sexual harassment.	☐	☐	☐
Discuss ways to avoid the pressure to cheat.	☐	☐	☐
Explain the purpose of the FERPA.	☐	☐	☐
Demonstrate the ability to effectively resolve a conflict.	☐	☐	☐

Steps to Achieve Unmet Objectives

Steps   Due Date

1. _____   _____

2. _____   _____

3. _____   _____

4. _____   _____

SUGGESTED ITEMS FOR LEARNING PORTFOLIO

▶ Ethical Research
▶ Conflict Resolution
▶ Legal Research

REFERENCES

Foothill College. (2005). Honor code. Retrieved October 4, 2005, from http://www.foothill.edu/services/honor.html

Kibler, L. & Vannoy Kibler, P. (1998). When students resort to cheating. In R. Holkeboer (Ed.), *College Success Reader*. Boston: Houghton

Mifflin. Retrieved February 25, 2005, from the State University of New York College at Cortland, Earth and Sky Web site: http://web.cortland.edu/earthandsky/Essays/Cheating.pdf

Penn Pulse State. (2000) (originally published in 1999). Academic integrity [Electronic version]. Retrieved February 25, 2005 from http://www.sa.psu.edu/sara/pulse/58-academic.PDF

Raimes, A. (1996). *Keys for Writers: A Brief Handbook*. Boston: Houghton Mifflin.

United States Department of Education. (n.d.) Family educational rights and privacy act (FERPA). Retrieved February 24, 2005, from http://www.ed.gov/policy/gen/guid/fpco/ferpa/index.html

United States Department of Education, Office for Civil Rights. (2004). Title IX grievance procedures, postsecondary education. Retrieved October 4, 2005, from http://www.ed.gov/about/offices/list/ocr/responsibilities_ix_ps.html

United States Department of Education, Office for Civil Rights. (2003). Annual report to Congress fiscal year 2003. Retrieved February 24, 2005, from http://www.ed.gov/about/offices/list/ocr/annrpt2003/report.html

United States Department of Justice. (2004). A guide to disability rights laws. Retrieved October 4, 2005, from the Americans with Disabilities Act Web site: http://www.ada.gov/cguide.htm

5

CHAPTER OUTLINE

6

Nutrition and Fitness Strategies for the Successful Student

CHAPTER

THE BIG PICTURE

LEARNING OBJECTIVES

By the end of this chapter, you will achieve the following objectives:

▶ Identify important components involved in achieving optimal health and energy.

▶ Explain the Dietary Guidelines for Americans and how they apply to personal health.

▶ Explain the major components of the MyPyramid guide and identify related health practices to optimize health and energy.

▶ Demonstrate the ability to use food package labels to make healthy food choices.

▶ Explain the importance of sufficient sleep and identify strategies for getting a good night's sleep.

▶ Define *good posture* and describe ergonomic positions related to student activities.

▶ List the criteria for an effective exercise program.

TOPIC SCENARIO

Alan is in his second year of college. He has a full-time job, family responsibilities, and difficult courses that require significant time spent studying. Alan often skips breakfast in order to get to his job, which starts at 7:30 a.m. He grabs a quick bite at one of the fast food places on his way from work to school. He often eats dinner out of the vending machine during the break between his 6:00 p.m. and 8:00 p.m. classes each evening. Alan works at a customer service call center during the day, sitting at the phone answering questions. When Alan gets home from his night classes, he spends at least two hours studying. He also studies for many hours on the weekends. Based on this short description of Alan's situation, answer the following questions:

▶ Reflect on your own daily schedule and work, family, and school responsibilities. How do Alan's challenges compare with your own situation?

▶ What specific health behaviors do you think Alan should be concerned with? List as many as you can identify from this short scenario. Read between the lines.

▶ Alan often complains of very low energy, difficulty in falling asleep at night, problems concentrating in class, and inability to rid himself of a nagging cold. What specific recommendations can you suggest to Alan to improve his energy, alertness, and preparation for his challenging responsibilities? What related questions do you need to have answered?

6

REFLECTION QUESTIONS

• Before moving on, how would you rate your own nutrition? In what areas do you think you do well? In what areas do you already know you need improvement?

• How would you rate your sleep? Do you regularly get a good night's sleep? Do you get the appropriate rest from work, school, and other life stresses?

• How would you rate your current level of fitness? In what areas are you satisfied? In what areas do you think you need improvement?

• Do you often have problems (aches, pains, muscle soreness, fatigue) that might be related to poor posture?

NUTRITION AND FITNESS: AN OVERVIEW

Positive health behaviors can significantly influence your success in school. Good nutrition can lead to better health, more energy, and higher levels of concentration. Optimal rest and sleep are important for optimal energy, reduction in fatigue, and the focus and attention required for effective and efficient learning. High levels of fitness and regular exercise can lead to positive health factors, a greater ability to relax and sleep well, and greater levels of attention. Good posture is an important part of fitness because it can help in alleviating the muscle soreness, aches and pains, and fatigue associated with long sessions of study, computer work, driving, or sitting in class. It is important for students to understand how to prioritize good nutrition, sleep, exercise, and posture for success in school.

NUTRITION: A KEY FACTOR IN HEALTH AND ENERGY LEVEL

Good nutrition is an essential element in good health, high energy, and focused attention. With the time and financial constraints facing students, practicing good nutrition behaviors can often seem impossible, yet a good diet may be a significant factor in school success and general health in the long run. A full discussion of nutrition is not possible in one chapter of a textbook. The goal here is to emphasize the importance of nutrition to school success, to highlight key elements of good nutrition, and to explain a few of the many tools available for helping you to make healthy food choices.

apply it

Three-Day Dietary Record

GOAL: To analyze your nutrient consumption to help in determining areas where your nutrition is optimal and areas where improvements could be made.

STEP 1: Schedule three consecutive days for your dietary record. Be sure that two of the days reflect normal work/school days and that the third day reflects a weekend day or day off. Try to choose days that will represent your typical diet behaviors.

STEP 2: Create a table similar to the example below and fill in each box with as much detail as possible. Include every food and beverage you consume.

Time	Food	Quantity	Activity/Feelings while eating

STEP 3: Using the MyPyramid guide (see the section on this later in this chapter), count the number of servings in each food group. Put a "+" by the serving if it is a healthy choice and a "−" by the serving if it is not a healthy choice.

STEP 4: Answer the following questions.

a. Did you meet the requirements suggested by the MyPyramid guide?

b. Were there food groups from which you ate significantly more or fewer servings as compared to the suggested servings?

c. Where needed, what substitutions could you make to improve your diet? Overall, how can you improve your diet?

? CRITICAL THINKING QUESTIONS

6–1. How do you think poor nutrition and fitness level can affect success in school or the workplace? List as many physiological, psychological, and emotional factors affected by nutrition and fitness as you can. Be very specific.

6–2. How do you think nutrition and fitness affect different age groups (i.e., children, adolescents, 20- to 30-year-olds, 40- to 50-year-olds, over 50, elderly)? List factors in detail.

6–3. What health factors later in life are affected by nutrition and fitness early in life? Be very specific (e.g., poor calcium intake early in life may lead to osteoporosis later in life).

6

Choosing meals that represent a healthy and balanced diet will provide you with the nutrition and energy needed for success in school.

DIETARY GUIDELINES FOR AMERICANS

The *Dietary Guidelines for Americans,* published by the U.S. Department of Health and Human Services (HHS) and the U.S. Department of Agriculture (USDA) (2005), present science-based dietary and physical activity behaviors designed to promote health and reduce the risk of chronic disease. The HHS and USDA work together to update these guidelines every few years based on the latest scientific findings. These suggestions recognize that good nutrition is essential for good health and that many of the leading causes of death and disease in Americans can be reduced or prevented entirely by practicing sound nutritional and physical fitness behaviors. Leading chronic diseases linked to poor diet or lack of physical activity include cardiovascular disease, hypertension, Type II diabetes, obesity, osteoporosis, diverticulitis, iron-deficiency anemia, oral disease, malnutrition, and some cancers.

MYPYRAMID

In spring 2005, the USDA released the revised food guidance system for Americans, MyPyramid. This new system expands the old food guide pyramid scheme to reflect the expanded guidelines for Americans, to give Americans options in their food choices, and to ensure that physical activity is emphasized in our daily lives.

Look carefully at the MyPyramid symbol on the next page. There are six important messages represented. First, *physical activity* is represented with the person on the steps, recognizing that exercise is essential for good health. *Proportionality* is represented by the different widths of the various food groups, emphasizing that we should consume different amounts from different groups. The narrowing of the food groups from bottom to top represents *moderation.* When you dig deeper into the pyramid information, you find that foods on the wider base of the pyramid include those with less added fats and sugars. Foods in the narrower top part of the pyramid are those with more added fats and sugars. These top foods should be consumed less than those in the base. *Variety* is represented in the pyramid by the different colors of the food group bands, recognizing that we should choose a variety of foods to consume a variety of nutrients. *Personalization* is a key to the new pyramid program. By exploring the www.mypyramid.gov more thoroughly, you can personalize a food and exercise plan to meet your individual needs. Finally, gradual improvement is highlighted in the slogan "Steps for a Healthier You," recognizing that improvements in health can be accomplished in gradual and small steps.

The MyPyramid Web site presents some basic messages for those desiring to improve their health through food choices and exercise. These basic messages are the same as those of the 2005 dietary guidelines. Along with basic messages, the MyPyramid Web site provides numerous tools to help in applying these messages. Review the site thoroughly to explore applying the information to your personal life.

FOOD PACKAGE LABELS: NUTRITION FACTS

The Nutrition Facts label found on food packages in the United States presents important information to help consumers determine healthy food choices. Read the entire package label to establish exactly what nutrients are contained in the food and how much of each nutrient is contained in each serving. Figure 6–1 explains each part of a Nutrition Facts label.

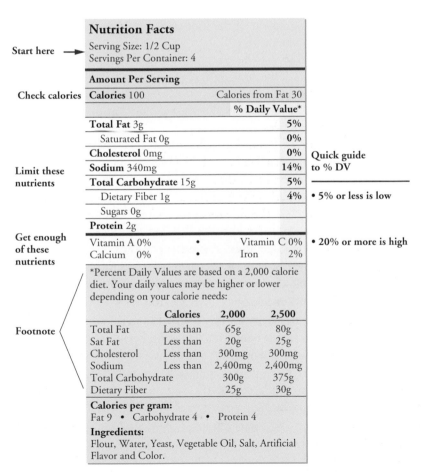

FIGURE 6–1.   Knowing how to read and interpret nutrition labels will allow you to make wise food choices.

6

The following packaging elements provide various facts about the food products that you purchase:

▶ **Front panel.** The front panel of any food container must say if any nutrient has been added or if any claim is being made about the food benefiting health. There are very strict guidelines about what a food manufacturer can put on a food label. Only a few health claims are allowed. These claims must be backed by substantial research. It is wise to think critically about any health claims that are presented.

▶ **Ingredient list.** The ingredient list tells if any substance has been added to the food in the package. Nutrients, fats, sugars, and other additives and preservatives are often added to foods to increase the nutritive value, to lengthen the shelf life, or to change the appearance or texture of the food. Ingredients are listed in descending order by weight. For example, if sugar is the first or second ingredient, it is a main ingredient of the food and should probably not be consumed in large quantities.

▶ **Nutrition facts.** This box on a food package is designed to help consumers compare foods to each other. There are several important elements on the Nutrition Facts label that nutrition-conscious consumers should understand.

  ▶ **Serving size:** Pay close attention to the serving size. All other values on the label are listed relative to this serving size. In other words, if the label says that there are five grams (g) of protein and the serving size is one cup, then for every cup of the food, there are 5 g of protein.

  ▶ **Servings per container:** This number says simply how many of the servings are in the entire container. Servings can be tricky. For example, if there are 220 calories per serving of juice and a bottle contains two servings, you are actually consuming 440 calories if you drink the entire bottle.

  ▶ **Calories and calories from fat:** This value tells how many calories there are in one serving. The label further states how many calories are specifically from fat.

  ▶ **Percent daily value (% DV):** This section tells the amount of major nutrients contained in each serving. The % DV tells the percent of the recommended daily intake of that nutrient (not the percent of the nutrient) in the food. Remember that all values are based on one serving of the amount indicated in the serving size notation.

  ▶ **Types of fat:** For foods containing fat, the amount of each kind of fat is listed. In general, monounsaturated fats are the best choice for good health. Many polyunsaturated fats are also good choices. Saturated fats are the poorest choice for good health. They are known to be a factor in atherosclerosis, high cholesterol, and heart disease.

▶ **Types of carbohydrate:** Carbohydrates are compounds including sugars, carbohydrates, and fiber. Carbohydrates and fiber are both important for good health. Foods high in sugars should be consumed on a limited basis.

▶ **Other nutrients:** If the food contains more than 2% DV of specific vitamins and minerals, the label must state the amount on the label. Remember that all amounts are based on the serving size. For example, if the label says 10% DV of vitamin A and the serving size is one cup, you must consume ten cups of the food to get 100% of the recommended amount of vitamin A, if this is the only food you are consuming.

▶ **Footnotes:** The footnotes provide reference information. Remember that each person is different. A highly active person might need to consume more than 2000 calories to maintain body weight. A very inactive person might need to consume fewer calories.

apply it

Food Package Label Activity

GOAL: To understand the correct use of the food package labels.

STEP 1: Organize into groups, if possible. Each person should collect five different packages of foods or beverages. Choose different types of foods and beverages and try to represent all food groups.

STEP 2: For each package, decide if the serving size on the package label represents the serving size typically eaten by a college student.

STEP 3: For each of the nutrients, determine which food/beverage has the greatest amount of nutrient by weight and percent daily value.

STEP 4: Using as many different foods as needed from the group of packages, create a nutritionally sound menu for one day. Try to create a menu that includes 100% of as many nutrients as possible and that you consider reasonable. Identify and discuss any deficiencies and solutions to repair these deficiencies.

▶ REFLECTION QUESTION

• Review some foods labels you have in your kitchen. What is your typical serving size for each food compared to the serving size used in food guides and package labels? Is there a difference, and, if so, how does it affect using these tools?

? CRITICAL THINKING QUESTIONS

6–4. What are common obstacles to healthy nutrition behaviors? List as many as you can. (These obstacles do not necessarily need to apply to you personally, but to the typical college student in a situation similar to yours.)

6–5. For each of these obstacles, what are at least two feasible solutions that you could recommend?

6

success steps

GUIDELINES FOR A HEALTHY DIET

1. Be aware of the nutritional value of the foods you eat.

2. Use scientifically based standards such as *Dietary Guidelines for Americans* and MyPyramid to guide your food choices.

3. Know how to read food labels to understand a food's nutritional value.

apply it

Three-Day Dietary Record #2

Repeat the Three-Day Dietary Record activity, incorporating any changes you have made to your diet after reading this section. Compare your energy levels, ability to concentrate, and general feelings of well-being between the two trials of the activity.

6

SLEEP: AN ESSENTIAL ACTIVITY FOR THE SUCCESSFUL STUDENT

The stresses associated with college are many and often overwhelming. These stresses, combined with normal and situational stresses of other areas of life, can have a negative impact on regular, sound sleep, which, in turn, negatively affects health, focus and attention, and the energy required to be a successful learner. It is estimated that adults need between seven and eight hours of sound sleep each night. The inability to fall asleep or stay asleep is termed *insomnia*. Insomnia can occur in people of all ages at different levels of severity and can cause sleep difficulties ranging from a few nights to many months in duration. Transient insomnia is when individuals have sleep difficulty for less than four weeks and is seen with excitement, stress, unfamiliar environments, and so forth. Short-term insomnia is defined as sleep difficulty for four weeks to six months. This kind of insomnia can be caused by long-term stress, psychiatric issues, or medical conditions. Chronic insomnia lasts more than six months and may be caused by physical problems.

© Digital Vision

Insufficient sleep can result in the need for naps during the day, which can negatively affect school performance.

CAUSES AND CONSEQUENCES OF INSUFFICIENT SLEEP

According to the Nebraska Rural Health and Safety Coalition (2002), there can be multiple possible causes of difficulties in sleeping:

- An inadequate amount of time devoted to sleep
- Factors that lead to poor-quality sleep (e.g., poor mattress, noisy environment, or a restless partner)
- Sleep disorders
- Excessive worry and preoccupation with life concerns
- Psychological factors and conditions, such as depression
- Disruption of the sleep schedule, caused by factors such as working at night or extensive travel
- Medical conditions that cause pain or other symptoms that interfere with sound and continuous sleep

The consequences of poor-quality or insufficient sleep include decreased alertness and attention, an inability to think and recall information clearly, and low energy, resulting in decreased performance and productivity in school. In addition, if you are working in a lab or shop, safety may be compromised. Most of the body can rest and recover during wakefulness in a relaxed state. However, the cerebral cortex part of the brain seems to need deep, nondreaming sleep. It is thought that the cerebral cortex requires the large, slow (delta) waves that occur during sleep. If deep sleep doesn't occur, skills are diminished. Studies by Harrison and Horne (1999, 2000) and Blagrove, Alexander, and Home (1995) suggest that impairment of decision making, effective communication, innovation, and memory all result from sleep deprivation. With long-term sleep deprivation, individuals become irritable, experience problems with relationships, and increase the risk for serious psychological disorders.

STRATEGIES FOR GOOD SLEEP

According to the American Academy of Sleep Medicine (2005), there are many things an individual can do to improve the likelihood of a good night's sleep or to overcome difficulties in falling asleep. Those who are struggling with falling asleep or not sleeping well can try any or all of the following recommendations to optimize sleep benefits:

- **Practice relaxation techniques before bedtime.** It is easier to fall asleep when one is relaxed. Relaxation helps relieve anxiety and tension that can hinder falling asleep quickly. Use relaxation techniques, play relaxing music, and avoid irritating interruptions to help in falling asleep.

6

▶ **Distract your mind before bedtime.** Consider reading a non-stressful book, watching nonstressful movies, or engaging in peaceful conversation before bedtime to distract the mind from the day's stress and challenges.

▶ **Take a hot bath just before bedtime.** Sleep naturally follows a sharp drop in body temperature; therefore, increasing body temperature with a hot bath may lead to sleep as the body returns to room temperature.

▶ **Create a quiet and peaceful environment.** Ensure that the environment is conducive to sleep, free of bright lights and sound (like the TV), and at the appropriate temperature (not too cold, hot, or stuffy).

▶ **Control the diet for sound sleep.** Avoid eating large meals right before bedtime, especially those high in fat. If a bedtime snack is necessary, choose foods higher in carbohydrates (i.e., breads, crackers, cereal). Avoid alcohol and caffeine right before bedtime. Caffeine is not only a stimulant, but it is also a diuretic. Consumption of caffeine within a few hours of bedtime will make it difficult to fall asleep, cause the sleep to be lighter, and increase the need to urinate, interrupting sound sleep. Though alcohol is classified as a depressant and may increase drowsiness, alcohol consumption before bedtime also leads to lighter sleep and waking up more frequently. Nicotine prior to bed can also hinder sound sleep.

▶ **Manage pain before bedtime.** Pain, even minor pain, can make it difficult to fall asleep and can wake a person often. Consider taking precautions to manage aches and pain before going to bed. Simple strategies include over-the-counter pain medication, heat, massage, and stretching. Obviously, those with serious or chronic pain should consult a physician.

▶ **Exercise daily.** Exercise early in the day (not close to bedtime) to help with falling asleep more easily and to support more sound sleep. Exercise right before bedtime can increase the metabolic rate, which makes falling asleep more difficult.

▶ **Keep the bedroom for sleeping.** Avoid working or watching TV in bed or using the bedroom for a study place or office, if possible. The brain might find it difficult to make the switch between work and rest. If falling asleep is difficult, consider moving to a different room and doing some quiet activity. Also, do not fall asleep outside of the bedroom (like on the couch in front of the TV).

▶ **Go to bed and get up at the same time each day.** Keeping a good sleep schedule can help train the body for regular, sound sleep.

▶ **Avoid napping in the daytime.** If drowsiness is preventing productive work, consider exercising. If a nap is unavoidable, sleep for no longer than a few minutes and do not nap late in the afternoon.

success steps

TIPS FOR BETTER SLEEP

1. Use relaxation techniques before bedtime.
2. Distract your mind from stressful thoughts before bedtime.
3. Take a hot bath.
4. Create a peaceful and quiet environment for sleep.
5. Choose a healthy diet, which contributes to sound sleep.
6. Address aches and pains that can interfere with sleep.
7. Get adequate exercise.
8. Avoid working and doing other activities in your bedroom. Reserve the bedroom for sleeping.
9. Keep a consistent sleep and waking schedule.
10. Don't take naps during the day.

EXERCISE: STRATEGIES FOR AVOIDING FATIGUE AND OPTIMIZING ENERGY

In addition to good nutrition and sleep, you can use regular exercise to help in avoiding fatigue, increasing focus and attention, improving energy levels, reducing risk for some diseases, and maintaining or improving overall health.

EXERCISE GUIDELINES

The American Academy of Family Physicians (2005) makes specific recommendations for physical activity:

▶ Engage in regular physical activity and reduce sedentary behavior to promote health, psychological well-being, and a healthy body weight.

▶ Achieve physical fitness by including cardiovascular conditioning, stretching exercises for flexibility, and resistance exercises or calisthenics for muscle strength and endurance.

! **RESOURCE BOX**

RESOURCES THAT CAN PROVIDE ADDITIONAL INFORMATION ON SLEEP
- American Academy of Sleep Medicine
- American Insomnia Association
- Conduct an Internet search using "sleep" as your search term.

▶ **REFLECTION QUESTIONS**

- What is your assessment of your sleep? Do you think you get sufficient sleep for optimal performance? How many hours of sleep do you get on average each night? What is the quality of your sleep?
- If your sleep is not optimal, what strategies do you think might work for you to improve the quantity and quality of your sleep?

6

? **CRITICAL THINKING QUESTION**

6–6. What might be the signs and symptoms of insufficient sleep in a college student? How specifically might these signs and symptoms be reflected in day-to-day school performance?

Regular exercise contributes to overall health by maintaining cardiovascular fitness, increasing muscle tone and flexibility, and relieving stress.

6

▶ Specifically, be physically active for at least 30 minutes most days of the week.

▶ Consult your physician on exercising for weight loss or if you have any medical conditions.

The President's Council on Physical Fitness and Sports (2006) further suggests strategies for safe aerobic activity:

▶ Warm up for 5 to 10 minutes before engaging in aerobic activity.

▶ Maintain exercise intensity for 30 to 45 minutes.

▶ Gradually decrease the intensity of the workout, then stretch to cool down during the last 5 to 10 minutes.

success steps

STEPS FOR EFFECTIVE EXERCISE

1. Select an exercise routine that you like and that you will engage in regularly.

2. Include exercises for both flexibility and cardiovascular fitness.

3. Engage in your exercise routine most days of the week.

4. Warm up before engaging in aerobic activity.

5. Sustain aerobic activity for 30 to 45 minutes.

6. Decrease intensity gradually and stretch to cool down.

COMPONENTS OF EXERCISE

According to the Centers for Disease Control and Prevention (2005), there are five major components of effective and safe exercise. Figure 6–2 shows examples of activities that can improve physical fitness.

▶ **Cardiorespiratory endurance.** Cardiorespiratory endurance describes how well the body brings in oxygen to the body, moves it to the blood for circulation throughout the body, and then distributes it among the body's cells for fuel utilization. The more active a person is, the greater his or her cardiorespiratory endurance needs to be. Improving cardiorespiratory endurance is accomplished by aerobic or endurance exercises such as biking, swimming, walking, running, and so forth.

▶ **Muscular strength.** Muscular strength describes how well the muscles exert force during activity. Improving muscular strength requires resistance exercises such as weight lifting.

▶ **Muscular endurance.** Muscular endurance describes how well muscles perform without fatiguing over a long period of activity.

FITNESS ACTIVITY BOX

Activity Intensity	Activities
Light Intensity	Walking slowly
	Golf, powered cart
	Swimming, slow treading
	Gardening or pruning
	Bicycling, very light effort
	Dusting or vacuuming
	Conditioning exercise, light stretching or warm-up
Moderate Intensity	Walking briskly
	Golf, pulling or carrying clubs
	Swimming, recreational
	Mowing lawn, power motor
	Tennis, doubles
	Bicycling 5 to 9 mph, level terrain or with a few hills
	Scrubbing floors or washing windows
	Weight lifting, resistance machines or free weights
Vigorous Intensity	Racewalking, jogging, or running
	Swimming laps
	Mowing lawn, hand mower
	Tennis, singles
	Bicycling more than 10 mph, or on steep uphill terrain
	Moving or pushing furniture
	Circuit training

FIGURE 6-2. Select the activity of appropriate intensity, based on your individual needs.

Some of the same activities that improve cardiorespiratory endurance also improve muscular endurance including running, biking, and swimming.

▶ **Body composition.** Body composition describes the relative amounts of bone, muscle, fat, and organs making up the body. A high level of body fat has been shown to increase the risk for many diseases, including heart disease, hypertension, joint disorders, and some cancers. Weight only describes one factor of body composition. Since muscle weighs more than fat, a person with well-developed muscles and low fat might weigh more and have a smaller size than a person with higher body fat. Lowering body fat can be accomplished by regular aerobic exercise and sound nutritional practices.

▶ **Flexibility.** Flexibility describes the range of motion of a joint. Flexible joints resist injury. Increasing the flexibility of joints is accomplished by safe stretching exercises.

! RESOURCE BOX

ADDITIONAL RESOURCES FOR FITNESS INFORMATION

• National Center for Chronic Disease Prevention and Health Promotion
• Healthy People 2010
• U.S. Department of Health and Human Services (HHS)
• National Institute of Diabetes and Digestive and Kidney Diseases (NDDK)
• The President's Council on Physical Fitness and Sports

▶ REFLECTION QUESTIONS

• How much do you currently exercise? In what areas do you think you might need to improve?
• Do you think you are at risk for any disease that might be prevented by increasing your exercise level? Describe these diseases and how exercise might lower the risk.

? CRITICAL THINKING QUESTION

6–7. What diseases can be prevented by regular exercise? How?

apply it

Exercise Program Research and Development

GOAL: To develop a safe and effective exercise program that can be utilized by a busy college student.

STEP 1: Connect to the Internet and search for aerobic, strength, and stretching exercises. Consider using these topics as your search terms.

STEP 2: Make a list of safety considerations you find in your research.

STEP 3: Design an exercise program that you personally will enjoy and that will fit into your student lifestyle. Include goals you have (e.g., weight loss, strength building, overall health maintenance, etc.). Use the examples in Figure 6–3 to help organize your program.

Time of day	Exercise details (Describe specifically the exercise you will do)	Number of repetitions or length of time dedicated to this exercise	Designated days in the week
6:00 am	Ride bike	25 minutes	M, W, F

FIGURE 6–3. Example of an exercise program plan.

POSTURE

In addition to exercise, posture is an essential component in good health. Poor posture can drain energy, cause fatigue, and increase the stress on the body. Good posture is defined as the position in which the bones are properly aligned so that joints, ligaments, and muscles can work in the way they were designed to work. Good posture allows the body's organs to rest in the proper position so that they can function normally. It also helps to strengthen the back muscles that maintain the natural curve of the spinal column, which helps to prevent or relieve lower back pain. Poor posture requires the muscles to work harder just to perform normal tasks and puts unnecessary and imbalanced stress on joints.

success steps

STEP BY STEP: ASSESSING GOOD POSTURE

Step 1: Stand in a relaxed position facing a mirror and wearing as few clothes as possible.

Step 2: Imagine a vertical line running down the body that goes exactly between the eyes and through the middle of the chin, collarbones, sternum, pubic bones, and midpoint between the ankles. This line should be vertical and straight from head to toe.

Step 3: Turn sideways to the mirror. Assess the curves made by your spinal column. You should see three natural curves: the cervical curve, the thoracic curve, and the lumbar curve. See Figure 6–4 for proper curvature.

Step 4: Face the mirror again. Imagine a horizontal line through each of the following pairs of joints: the shoulders, the hips, and the knees. Each horizontal line should be perfectly straight and parallel to the ground.

Step 5: Assess the head while relaxed. It should be perfectly straight, as though it were floating on top of the spinal column, not tilting to either side.

Step 6: Solicit help from a friend, camera, or video recording. From the back, assess the vertebrae. The spinal process forming the bumps on each side of the vertebral column should be straight and even down the entire spinal column.

Poor posture can result from several factors:

◗ Injuries

◗ Poor sleep support (a poor-quality mattress)

◗ Excessive weight

◗ Visual deficiencies

◗ Foot problems and improper shoes

◗ Weak muscles and muscle imbalance

◗ Careless sitting, standing, and sleeping habits

◗ Occupational stress (including working on a computer)

◗ Poorly designed workspace

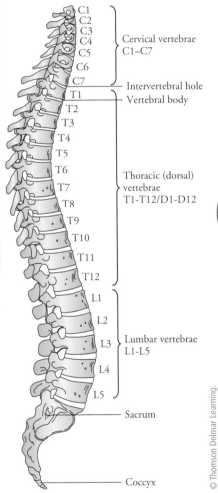

© Thomson Delmar Learning.

FIGURE 6–4. Maintaining the natural curves of the spinal column contributes to good posture and health.

6

Poor posture can cause and contribute to health difficulties as well as general fatigue. Consider the following possible consequences of poor posture:

▶ **Reduced oxygen intake and compromised circulation.** In order to function optimally, the lungs must be able to inflate and deflate adequately. Slumped posture impedes the lungs' ability to expand and contract, resulting in shallow breathing. Consequently, the amount of oxygen available to body tissues via normal circulation is reduced, resulting in fatigue and less than optimal function of body systems.

▶ **Joint and muscular pain.** Poor posture can cause misalignment of joints, placing unnatural pull and pressure on muscles. The result can be chronic muscular pain, such as in the low back.

▶ **Nerve dysfunction.** The nerves that supply the body exit the spinal cord through the vertebrae, the small bones that make up the spinal column. Nerves travel throughout the body to muscles and tissues and control movement as well as organ function. A misaligned spinal column or pressure on a muscle or organ due to poor posture can compress nerves and impair their function.

▶ **Improper digestive and bowel function.** The digestive and excretory systems rely on wave-like movements to propel food and waste through the respective systems. Poor posture inhibits the natural movements of these systems and can interfere with healthy digestion and elimination.

▶ **Serious medical conditions.** Poor posture that causes chronic compression of muscles, nerves, or other systems can result in serious medical conditions. Many people are familiar with carpal tunnel syndrome (CTS), which causes compression of the nerves in the wrist, resulting in pain, tingling, and numbness of the hands. In serious cases, surgery is required to correct the problem. In many cases, attention to posture and ergonomics can prevent CTS.

Maintaining good posture requires paying attention to how you sit, walk, lift and carry items, and sleep. Consider the following suggestions for improving your posture:

▶ Keep body weight within normal ranges.

▶ Sleep on a firm mattress of high quality.

▶ Get regular eye exams and resolve vision problems.

▶ Create a work environment conducive to good posture.

▶ Be aware of ergonomic principles and apply them to your daily activities.

▶ Focus on good posture until it becomes an unconscious habit.

▶ When standing, hold head high with chin forward, shoulders back, chest out, and stomach tucked in.

▶ When sitting, use a chair with a firm seat and low back support, keep table top at elbow height, and keep knees a little higher than hips.

▶ When working on a computer, position the screen 10 to 15 degrees below eye level and put reference materials even with and close to the monitor.

▶ When studying or working at a desk, stand up, move around, rest the eyes, and do stretches every 20 minutes or so.

▶ When sleeping, sleep on your side with knees bent and head supported by a pillow or on your back with a small pillow supporting neck. Avoid sleeping on your back with bulky pillows under the head.

• Top of monitor just below eye level. This supports keeping the head over the shoulders. Comfortable viewing is generally 5 to 30 degrees below horizontal. Place in front of the body to prevent sitting in a twisted posture or turning the head.

• Head over the shoulders to allow the skeleton to carry the weight of the head, relieving overuse of neck, shoulder, and back muscles.

• Monitor distance so that chin doesn't jut forward while the trunk is against the chair back.

• Seat back should support curve in lower (lumbar) spine. Higher seat backs are recommended to relieve spinal pressures. A slight backward angle is preferred to allow the chair to take some load off the spine. Allow the chair to carry a share of the body weight.

• Keyboard height should allow for relaxed shoulders, flat wrists, and at least ninety degrees at the inside of elbow. Sit directly in front, close enough not to have to reach forward. Rest palms on rest only when fingers can remain relaxed.

• Armrests, if used, soft and wide. There should be no contact during keying. Close enough to not force extension of elbows, and low enough for shoulders to be relaxed without slumping or leaning.

• Thighs level with or just above knees to promote a neutral spine.

• Seat pan not so deep that comfortable contact with chair back is prevented. Contact behind the knees must be avoided. Optimal contact with thighs provides greatest degree of effortless support.

• Feet in firm contact with the floor to distribute load through the whole body. Use a footrest only if necessary. Leave space under desk free of any obstruction to legs.

FIGURE 6-5. Ergonomics is the study of effective positioning of work-related tasks. Ergonomic workstations position tools and equipment so that good posture and body alignment are maintained.

REFLECTION QUESTIONS

- Do you often feel sore spots anywhere on your body?
- How often do you take breaks from studying to move around, stretch, and rest your eyes?
- What is your typical position when sitting, standing, working on a computer, and walking? (Take a look at your posture critically and in the mirror and describe specifically what you see. Start with your head and assess each joint, the alignment and evenness of joint pairs, and each segment of your body as a unit.)

? CRITICAL THINKING QUESTION

6–8. For each of the following body areas, how might poor posture specifically affect the area and what should be done to improve posture in that area? Give specific examples that might be common for students and give easy solutions. Consider shoulders, lower back, knees, and head/neck.

6

success steps

IMPROVING YOUR POSTURE

1. Set an alarm to go off every 20 or 30 minutes during long study sessions as a reminder to take a quick break and stretch.

2. Using a search tool such as Google, search the Internet for stretching exercises. Select ones you like and incorporate them into your study sessions.

3. If you have problems with posture, try to develop the habit of checking your posture several times throughout the day while walking, sitting, driving, and so forth.

CHAPTER SUMMARY

This chapter focused on the importance of physical considerations, such as nutrition, exercise, sleep, and posture, to your daily functioning. If you compare how well you function when you are feeling your best to when you are ill or fatigued, the significance of maintaining your health may become more apparent.

The demands of school, which are typically in addition to other life responsibilities, require endurance, clear thinking, and energy. Sound health practices, such as those described in this chapter, become the foundation for success in carrying out all of your responsibilities effectively. Good health lays the foundation for success in all of the areas discussed in *100% Student Success*.

POINTS TO KEEP IN MIND

In this chapter, several main points were discussed in detail:

- ❱ Nutrition and fitness are critical to good health, high energy, and the focus and attention needed to be a successful student.
- ❱ The *Dietary Guidelines for Americans* and the MyPyramid guide serve as excellent guides for good food choices.
- ❱ Knowing how to read food package labels also helps in making good food choices and in comparing foods for purchase.

❱ Sleep is an essential part of good health and success as a student. There are several strategies that can be used to increase the quality and quantity of sleep and to avoid the problems associated with poor or insufficient sleep.

❱ Exercise is essential for good health, and the benefits of regular exercise are important for the successful student.

❱ Posture is an important component of fitness and good health. Good posture can help students avoid aches, pains, and fatigue associated with long study sessions.

LEARNING OBJECTIVES REVISITED

Review the learning objectives for this chapter and rate your level of achievement for each objective using the rating scale provided. For each objective on which you do not rate yourself as a 3, outline a plan of action that you will take to fully achieve the objective. Include a time frame for this plan.

1 = did not successfully achieve objective

2 = understand what is needed, but need more study or practice

3 = achieved learning objective thoroughly

	1	2	3
Identify important components involved in optimal health and energy.	☐	☐	☐
Explain the Dietary Guidelines for Americans and how they apply to personal health.	☐	☐	☐
Explain the major components of the MyPyramid guide and identify related health practices to optimize health and energy.	☐ ☐	☐ ☐	☐ ☐
Demonstrate the ability to use food package labels to make food choices.	☐	☐	☐
Explain the importance of sufficient sleep and identify strategies for getting a good night's sleep.	☐ ☐	☐ ☐	☐ ☐
Define *good posture* and describe ergonomic positions related to activities involved in being a student.	☐	☐	☐
List the criteria for an effective exercise program.	☐	☐	☐

Steps to Achieve Unmet Objectives

Steps	Due Date
1. _____	_____
2. _____	_____
3. _____	_____
4. _____	_____

SUGGESTED ITEMS FOR LEARNING PORTFOLIO

▶ Three-Day Dietary Records
▶ Food Package Label Activity
▶ Exercise Program Research and Development

REFERENCES

American Academy of Family Physicians. (2005). Exercise: A healthy habit to start and keep. Retrieved May 5, 2005, from http://familydoctor.org/059.xml

American Academy of Sleep Medicine. (2005). Other Resources – Fact Sheet. Retrieved March 11, 2005, from http://www.aasmnet.org/FactSheet.aspx

Blagrove, M., Alexander, C., & Horne, J. (1995). The effects of chronic sleep reduction on the performance of cognitive tasks sensitive to sleep deprivation. *Applied Cognitive Psychology, 9*(1), 21–40.

Centers for Disease Control and Prevention. (2005). Physical activity for everyone: Components of physical fitness. Retrieved October 5, 2005, from http://www.cdc.gov/nccdphp/dnpa/physical/components/index.htm

Department of Health and Human Services and the U.S. Department of Agriculture. (2005). Dietary Guidelines for Americans 2005. Retrieved March 11, 2005, from http://www.healthierus.gov/dietaryguidelines

Harrison, Y., & Horne, J. (1999). One night of sleep loss impairs innovative thinking and flexible decision making. *Organizational Behavior and Human Decision Processes, 78*(2), 128–145.

Harrison, Y., & Horne, J. (2000). The impact of sleep deprivation on deci-
    sion making: A review. *Journal of Experimental Psychology – Applied,*
    6(3), 236–249.

Nebraska Rural Health and Safety Coalition. (2002). Sleep Deprivation:
    Causes and Consequences. Retrieved March 11, 2005, from the
    Centers for Disease Control and Prevention, National Ag Safety
    Database Web site: http://www.cdc.gov/nasd/docs/d000701-
    d000800/d000705/d000705.html

President's Council on Physical Fitness and Sports. (2006). Fitness
    fundamentals: Guidelines for personal exercise programs. Retrieved
    May 5, 2006, from http://www.fitness.gov/fitness.htm

6

CHAPTER OUTLINE

Finances and College

Financial Resources for College

Major Purchases and Buying Insurance

Planning Finances beyond College

7

Financial Considerations for School Success

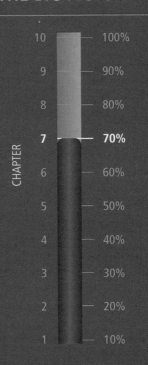

THE BIG PICTURE

LEARNING OBJECTIVES

By the end of this chapter, you will achieve the following objectives:

▶ Describe general financial considerations that must be made during college attendance.

▶ Discuss management of credit.

▶ Discuss elements to consider when making major purchases.

▶ Define various forms of financial assistance and locate resources for each.

▶ Be able to determine a workable budget based on recommended budgeting principles.

▶ Explain basic financial investments and the advantages and disadvantages of each.

TOPIC SCENARIO

Paul McGuire is beginning his second semester of college. Paul's first semester was difficult for him financially. He never seemed to have enough money to purchase necessities such as food and rent, let alone extras such as entertainment and recreational activities. As a result, Paul has accumulated some credit card debt on several cards that he carries. He is looking forward to planning the remainder of his college education, but he is beginning to develop concerns about his finances. Paul receives some financial aid, but it appears that he may need additional funding. He works 25–30 hours per week in addition to attending classes.

Based on Paul's situation, answer the following questions:

▶ What strategies might Paul use in establishing a budget?

▶ What advice would you give to Paul regarding the use of credit cards?

▶ What might Paul do to supplement his financial aid? From what sources might he seek reliable information?

▶ How might Paul's employer be of assistance in Paul's financial planning?

FINANCES AND COLLEGE

Financing college can be a challenge for anyone, although the type of challenge may be different depending on individual circumstances such as age, outside commitments, and other individual factors. Existing financial obligations and concerns can be complicated by emergencies and other unexpected events.

SOUND, INDIVIDUALIZED FINANCIAL ADVICE

The importance of sound financial advice personalized to your specific circumstances cannot be overstated. It is critical to remember that finances are an individual issue and it is not possible to make general statements that will apply to everyone. The information presented in this chapter is intended as *guidelines only* and should be treated as a starting point from which to develop your own personalized plan. Consult with your school's financial aid personnel, your accountant, banker, parents, and other qualified financial advisors for information specifically customized to your individual needs.

PERSONAL FINANCES

Personal finances are influenced by several factors. Existing financial commitments, availability of financial support, and financial demands that occur during the course of school are factors to consider. Housing and related expenses, food, and other costs in addition to the cost of school can put significant strain on personal finances. Managing personal finances generally takes careful planning and discipline; this may be even more true with the added costs of college. Young Money (2002a) offers the following suggestions in its "Financial Basics for College Students": Have a spending plan, manage credit responsibly, and understand the use of various accounts as strategies for managing personal finances.

Balancing personal and life expenses while going to school requires effective planning and budgeting.

apply it

Budgeting Resources on the Web

GOAL: *To become familiar with budgeting resources and strategies and select an effective approach to budgeting based on individual needs.*

STEP 1: Conduct an Internet search using "budgeting tools" or "creating budgets" as your search term. There are many free options available.

STEP 2: Select a tool that fits your needs and that you will be comfortable using.

STEP 3: Use the tool for a month or two. Review your budgeting at the end of the time period to determine the tool's effectiveness. Make adjustments and changes as needed.

REFLECTION QUESTION

- What techniques and strategies do you use to manage your personal finances?

7

A Spending Plan

A spending plan is similar to a budget. A spending plan allows you to determine the amount of money that you have available, track how your money is being spent, and make adjustments according to your needs. The article "Putting a Spending Plan Together" at Young Money (2002b) suggests the following steps:

success steps

CREATING A SPENDING PLAN AND BUDGET

Step 1: Know your income and expenses. Collect all receipts, bank account records, invoices, income statements, and other documents related to spending and income. Create categories that fit your specific needs and spending patterns. Based on the documentation that you gathered, estimate the amount of money that you spend on each category per month.

Step 2: Determine your annual income from all sources. Divide that figure by 12 to arrive at your monthly income.

Step 3: Determine monthly amounts to spend on each category of expenses. Although these amounts may vary somewhat based on individual need, these percentages represent recommended proportions of total income that can be allocated to expense categories. Consider the following recommended guidelines:

- Housing: 23–33%

- Life/car insurance: 4–6%

- Food: 12–20%

- Charities: 5–10%

- Transportation: 7–10%

- Personal debt repayment: 8–18%

- Entertainment/recreation: 4–6%

- Clothing: 4–7%

- Savings: 5–10%

- Medical: 3–5%

Remember that these are suggested amounts and should be used as guidelines. You may need to modify them by adding categories or adjusting the figures. Use your own best judgment and advice from your financial advisor to determine precise budgeting for your circumstances. The goal of this step is to gain perspective on your total income and determine the amount of money that you realistically have for each category of expenses.

Step 4: Understand your spending patterns. Keep receipts, check stubs or register, and other records of payments and purchases that you make. Use an expense tracking chart, plain notebook, or software program to track your expenses. Choose a method with which you are comfortable and that you will use consistently.

Step 5: Each month, compare your spending to the plan you have set. If there are major inconsistencies in your plan and actual spending patterns, assess where you can make adjustments. Determine whether long-term or short-term changes need to be made. You may need to make modifications to your overall spending habits or to accommodate a one-time expense, such as a car repair.

Step 6: Keep track of your spending and your plan. A monthly review of your spending compared to your plan will allow you to understand your spending habits and budget according to your needs.

Step 7: Build your monthly budget based on your spending plan and needs. Implement methods for staying within the budget that was determined by your spending plan.

apply it

Budget Activity

GOAL: *To establish a monthly budget.*

STEP 1: Prepare a ledger. The ledger should contain a column for where bills are listed, amounts due, and due dates. Include columns for listing categories such as entertainment, groceries, clothes, medical bills, etc.

STEP 2: On the ledger, list the dates of incoming monies in one column.

STEP 3: Fill out each column correctly, indicating all bill amounts and amounts that are typically spent on a monthly basis.

STEP 4: Determine if all areas have been covered and if enough money is available on a monthly basis. If there is a lack of money for all the bills, analyze areas that might be consolidated. Call companies as needed to determine if this is possible.

STEP 5: Readjust the ledger as decisions are made regarding due dates and consolidation.

STEP 6: If money is remaining after all bills have been paid, determine if some bills such as credit cards can be paid off more quickly. Adjust these payments and payoff dates on the ledger as determined.

7

Part of your personal spending plan will include how you use credit. Use credit wisely to establish a strong financial record for the future.

Limiting Credit

One of the recommended methods for staying within your spending plan is to limit your opportunities to use credit. Young Money (2002a) suggests using only one credit card and requesting a low credit limit. Contact your credit card company to adjust your credit limit. If you have a balance on your card, you may also consider negotiating a lower interest rate. Interest charges on a balance add up, and credit card companies will often reduce interest rates to keep your business. Research the current interest rates so that you can speak from an informed position.

apply it

Credit Research

GOAL: To become aware of responsible credit use and the consequences of its abuse.

STEP 1: Conduct an Internet search using "credit" or "use of credit cards" as your search term.

STEP 2: Look in the results for documents that explain the responsible use of credit and the consequences of abusing it.

STEP 3: Based on your findings, determine any changes to your credit practices that you believe to be important. Set goals and select methods for implementing these changes.

Online Banking

Online banking allows you to closely monitor your money by offering access to your financial records 24 hours a day, seven days a week. Online banking allows you to track debits and credits on a daily basis and may include features such as electronic bill paying, transfer of funds between accounts, and other additional services. If you choose to use features such as electronic bill payments, you can access the majority of your records in one place, which provides more efficient recordkeeping as well as greater convenience.

Check Registers and Ledgers

A paper check ledger gives you immediate access to your account information when the Internet is not available. Keeping an accurate and current check register allows you to track your expenditures and know exactly where your spending was as well as track the amount of your available funds. Recording each check as it is written lets you know what checks have been written but have not yet cleared the bank.

Building a Strong Credit History

Manage your finances in a manner that builds a strong credit history. A strong credit history is created by paying credit card balances monthly and may allow you to qualify for other and often more major loans (such as a mortgage) later on (Duguay, 2003; Schmidgall, 2002). Experts also warn against the credit card offers that college students frequently receive and emphasize the importance of using credit responsibly. Use credit in accordance with your spending plan. The important concept to remember and put into practice is that establishing credit is important in today's world, but abusing it can lead to serious consequences. Using good judgment (and sometimes restraint!) is a key factor in achieving this balance.

FINANCIAL RESOURCES FOR COLLEGE

There are many resources that students use to pay for college, including personal savings and income, parents' savings and income, and financial aid, such as loans, grants, scholarships, and work-study. The types of financing one can receive depend largely on individual situations.

FINANCIAL AID

CollegeData.com (2004a) defines financial aid as "any form of assistance that helps you and your family cover the costs of attending college." There are numerous sources for financial aid, and the source that you use will depend again on your individual situation.

Qualifying and Applying for Financial Aid

Regardless of what you believe your financial situation to be, it is wise to apply for financial aid (CollegeData.com, 2004b). Because of the many factors that are used to calculate eligibility for financial aid, you may qualify for some type of assistance, regardless of your financial circumstances. Be aware that financial aid is available for students already enrolled in college, as long as published application deadlines are met. Financial aid is not only for high school students applying to college for the first time.

? **CRITICAL THINKING QUESTIONS**

7–1. What are some areas in which you could improve or revise your budgeting and spending patterns?

7–2. Where might you seek additional assistance and information?

7

© 2005 JupiterImages Corporation

Financial aid personnel at your school and elsewhere can help you budget and finance your college education.

Financial aid typically comes from the federal or state governments, the colleges themselves, or private sources such as banks and private organizations. To determine individual eligibility, sources of financial assistance use the Free Application for Federal Student Aid (FAFSA). The FAFSA is a tool used by the U.S. Department of Education to analyze individual financial need based on uniform standards. To learn more about financial aid and the FAFSA, conduct an Internet search using "United States Department of Education" as your search term, find the federal government Web site for the Department of Education, and explore the many options for information that you find.

The following suggestions for completing the FAFSA and implementing the application process efficiently and effectively come from CollegeData.com's "Tips for your financial aid forms" (2004c):

1. **Read all instructions and review the form first.** The FAFSA instructions contain information that can influence how you complete the form and that may affect your eligibility for aid. For example, certain words are defined in specific ways, and using the wrong word may change the meaning of the information you provide.

2. **Plan ahead.** As you read through the instructions, note deadlines on your calendar. Be aware of details such as whether the deadline is a postmark date or the date the paperwork needs to be received. You will need to plan accordingly and allow ample time for mailing if you are not completing the form electronically. (Even if you are using the electronic submission option, it is wise to allow extra time in case of transmission problems.)

3. **Write legibly and fill in all the blanks.** If you can type your application, do so. If not, write clearly in dark (preferably black) ink. It is wise to print an extra copy of the paperwork and complete a draft before completing the final copy for submission. If something does not apply to you, mark "N/A" to indicate that it is not applicable or indicate this as instructed on the form. Leaving the item blank could be interpreted as a missed item and could delay the processing of your application.

4. **Review the completed form.** After the form is completed, read it over to ensure that you have answered questions thoroughly and provided complete information. Allow enough time in the planning process to let the completed form to sit for a day or two after completion. You may be more objective and focused when you return to the form after taking some time off.

5. **Keep copies for consistency.** Keep copies of all completed forms and correspondence related to the financial aid application

process. Use your copies as a reference for completing future financial aid documentation. This will ensure that the information that you provide is consistent and eliminate the need to research the information a second time, except for necessary updates. The copy will also serve as a reference for you in the event you need to clarify or resubmit any information. Discard any draft copies and retain only the copy of the final version to eliminate confusion.

success steps

COMPLETING FINANCIAL AID FORMS

1. Read all instructions and review the form first.
2. Plan ahead. Note important deadlines on your calendar.
3. Write legibly and fill in all the blanks. Write "N/A" (not applicable) if the item does not apply to you.
4. Review the completed form.
5. Keep copies for reference.

> **REFLECTION QUESTION**
>
> • How efficiently do you complete financial aid and related paperwork?

Types of Financial Aid

Eligibility for financial aid is determined on the basis of need or merit. Need is determined by the difference between the cost of attending college less the amount that you are expected to contribute, based on analysis of the information on your FAFSA. Merit is determined by your performance and achievement record in academics and other areas. Some types of financial aid use a combination of these criteria to determine eligibility (College-Data.com, 2004a).

See Figure 7–1 for an overview of your financial aid options. Financial aid comes in the following types:

> **CRITICAL THINKING QUESTION**
>
> 7–3. What strategies could you implement to make your financial aid and related paperwork more efficient?

7

▶ **Grants.** Grants are given according to need and include Pell Grants, Federal Supplemental Educational Opportunity Grants (FSEOG), and others. Each type of grant has its own criteria for eligibility as well as maximum amounts that can be awarded. Grants are based on need and do not have to be repaid.

▶ **Loans.** Loans are also based on need and, as is the case with grants, there are several types, each with its own eligibility requirements and criteria for repayment. Loans can come from the government or from private lenders and must be repaid with interest. All loans are obtained by signing a legally binding agreement.

TYPES OF FINANCIAL AID

Type of Aid	Examples	General Parameters
Grants	▶ Pell grants ▶ Federal Supplemental Educational Opportunity Grants (FSEOG)	▶ Based on need ▶ Each grant has its own criteria for eligibility ▶ Each grant has its own maximum amount that can be awarded ▶ Does not have to be repaid
Loans	▶ Government loans ▶ Private loans	▶ Based on need ▶ Each has its own eligibility requirements ▶ Each has its own criteria for repayment ▶ Must be repaid with interest ▶ Obtained by signing a legally binding agreement
Scholarships	▶ Awarded by individual colleges ▶ Awarded by private sources	▶ Based on scholastic or other achievement ▶ Does not have to be repaid ▶ May be designated for particular groups or have other specific requirements
Work-Study Programs	▶ Offer students an opportunity to work on or off campus while attending school ▶ Federal government program that may be subsidized by states or private industry	▶ Student earns a salary for specific job ▶ Usually based on need ▶ Earnings are not repaid
Other Options	▶ Internships ▶ Education cooperatives ▶ Other programs that provide an opportunity to work for wages while completing your education	▶ Less common than other forms of financial aid ▶ Specifics depend on the program

FIGURE 7–1. Having a working knowledge of financial aid options will help you to know what is available to you and guide you in asking appropriate questions of financial aid personnel.

Adapted from the U.S. Department of Education (2006) and CollegeData.com.

It is important to understand the difference between a subsidized and unsubsidized loan. A subsidized loan is one that is awarded based on financial need, and interest on the loan does not accrue until loan repayment begins after graduation. The loan is subsidized in that the federal government pays interest while you are in school. Conversely, an unsubsidized loan requires that you pay interest on the loan from the time you first receive funds until the loan is fully repaid. Interest on unsubsidized loans is capitalized, so you are required to pay interest on any interest that accrues. Some students choose to pay the interest as it accrues to minimize extra expense (California State University–Sacramento, n.d.).

▶ **Scholarships.** Scholarships are generally awarded by individual colleges or private sources. They are traditionally based on scholastic achievement and do not have to be repaid. Some scholarships are designated for particular groups or have other specific requirements that must be met. For example, some agencies that provide scholarships require the recipient to work for the agency for a designated amount of time following graduation.

▶ **Work-study programs.** Work-study programs offer students an opportunity to work on or off campus while attending school. The government pays a part of the salary. Work-study programs are typically part of federal financial aid, but may be subsidized by the state or college in some situations.

▶ **Other options.** Other possibilities for financial assistance include internships, education cooperatives, and other programs that provide an opportunity to work for wages while completing your education. Although these programs are less common than other forms of financial aid, they are available in some situations and can be viable options for some students.

Finding Specific Resources

There are several resources for researching financial aid options. Financial aid information is available from your campus financial aid department, your college or public library, or by conducting an Internet search (United States Department of Education, n.d.). There are services that charge for searching for financial aid information. Free information is available, so if you do choose a service that charges a fee, get a clear indication of what the fee covers.

▶ REFLECTION QUESTION

- How knowledgeable are you about financial aid options?

? CRITICAL THINKING QUESTIONS

7–4. Have you utilized all of the financial aid options available to you?
7–5. What do you need to do to become more knowledgeable about your choices?
7–6. Where can you find the best information for your needs?

7

MAJOR PURCHASES AND BUYING INSURANCE

As an adult student, it is possible that you will make a major purchase during your college career. Major purchases such as automobiles, homes, and insurance require sound planning and wise choices.

RENTING A HOME

There are several elements to consider when preparing to rent a house or apartment. Both you and the landlord have rights that are often defined by local law and of which you should be aware before signing a lease or rental agreement. The American Institute of Certified Public Accountants (AICPA) makes the following suggestions for renting a house or apartment:

▶ **Understand the terms of your lease.** It is important that you know if you will be able to negotiate leaving before the lease expires. If so, find out whether there are penalties, what they are, and if you can sublet the property. What are the terms of a standard lease in your locale?

▶ **Understand the finances.** An important part of the terms of the lease is knowing the date rent is due and the penalties for late payment. In addition, find out the amount of the security deposit and the conditions for its return. Know whether first and last month's rent is required in addition to the security deposit.

▶ **Know the legalities affecting rental properties in your area.** Local laws affect your rights as a renter. Contact your city government for information on housing regulations in your area. For example, some locales have limits on rent increases. You should be informed of these types of restrictions for your own protection. If it is not clear which specific office to contact, the general information office should be able to direct you to the appropriate department.

▶ **Understand inclusions, exclusions, and restrictions.** Find out what utilities and maintenance charges are included in the rent as well as rules regarding pets and children. Ask if there are restrictions on decorating and painting. Know the hours during which management and maintenance personnel are available and what their responsibilities include. Find out what facilities (such as laundry and recreation) are available on the premises and their hours of operation. Ask about parking restrictions such as limitations on number of vehicles and guest parking.

▶ **Dispute resolution.** Find out how disputes with the landlord are typically addressed. Is there a defined dispute resolution protocol for both renter and landlord? Are you entitled to arbitration?

success steps

RENTING A HOME

1. Understand the terms of your lease.
2. Understand the finances.
3. Know the legalities affecting rental properties in your area.
4. Understand inclusions, exclusions, and restrictions.
5. Learn the process for dispute resolution.

PURCHASING A HOME

Purchasing a home can be an exciting yet somewhat intimidating process. Purchasing a home provides you with an investment and can be a tax benefit. It is important to understand the major considerations of purchasing a home and to know where to seek sound professional advice in the process. The U.S. Department of Housing and Urban Development (HUD) makes the following recommendations and suggestions for home buyers (2003, 2005):

▶ **Investigate your loan options.** There are many choices for obtaining a loan for the purchase of a home. HUD recommends shopping around as you would for any major purchase to find the best rate on loans. If you are in a situation such as having a poor credit history, a minimal amount for a down payment, or other extenuating circumstances, contact the HUD offices, as options may be available for you.

▶ **Be a wise shopper.** Learn about the home purchasing process by taking a HUD course in home ownership. Know relative values and investigate the prices of homes in the neighborhood and surrounding areas to ensure that you are getting a comparable value. Follow HUD guidelines for completing loan applications to avoid loan fraud. Contact HUD for more detailed information on protecting yourself in the loan acquisition process.

▶ **Seek the assistance of professionals.** A professional real estate agent understands the intricacies of home buying and can advise you on elements such as financial issues, the area in which you plan to purchase your home, and other aspects of the transaction. The fees for the broker come from the home seller—not the buyer—so having a professional real estate broker does not add to your costs, yet is a valuable service. Seek a certified home inspector to inspect any home that you are considering purchasing, to ensure that it is in good condition. HUD also recommends interviewing several professionals and checking their references before selecting the broker with whom you choose to work.

▶ **Know your expenses.** It is important to be aware of the costs, such as earnest money, down payments, and closing costs that are associated with home purchase. These costs can vary, depending on your situation. Again, a professional real estate broker can help you understand these fees and work with you to achieve a plan that fits your needs.

Your best option is to work with knowledgeable professionals and agencies when making a major purchase such as a house.

Making a major purchase requires planning carefully, knowing your options, and understanding all related expenses.

success steps

PURCHASING A HOME

1. Investigate your loan options. Know which loan choice is best for you.

2. Be a wise shopper. Consider taking a course in home buying, such as those offered by HUD (Housing and Urban Development).

3. Seek the assistance of professionals, such as a knowledgeable real estate agent.

4. Know your expenses. Be aware of the costs associated with purchasing a home.

PURCHASING AN AUTOMOBILE

Many of the considerations in purchasing an automobile are similar to those in buying a house. Consider the following guidelines when buying a vehicle (AICPA, 2004a):

▶ **Weigh leasing versus buying.** Although many people favor leasing over purchasing, leasing is not always the best option. Besides the fact that you will not actually own the vehicle, there may be additional fees associated with leasing. Check your options carefully and compare leasing to a variety of loan options.

▶ **Shop around for a loan.** Investigate several sources for loans to find the best rate possible. Possible sources for loans include banks, credit unions, and other lending institutions, as well as the car manufacturer itself.

▶ **Know the terms of the agreement.** Have a clear understanding of the terms and conditions of the loan or lease. Make sure that the agreement addresses issues such as prepayment options and penalties and the length of the loan or lease. Ensure that the amount of the loan is appropriate for the age of the vehicle.

success steps

PURCHASING AN AUTOMOBILE

1. Weigh the benefits and costs of buying versus leasing.

2. Find the best loan—shop around.

3. Know the terms of the lease or loan.

4. Ensure that the terms of the loan are appropriate for the age of the car.

PURCHASING INSURANCE

There are many types of insurance, such as health, home, and automobile. Insurance regulations typically vary by state, and your best information regarding insurance purchases is likely to come from your state insurance commissioner's office. The following are general guidelines regarding different types of insurance. As with any major purchase, you are wise to educate yourself about your options and the reputation of the professional with whom you are dealing.

▶ **Health insurance.** Major medical insurance policies can protect you in the event of a major illness or medical need. General policies may include office visits, optical care, and other benefits. Your choice will depend on your needs. Schools sometimes offer insurance options at reasonable prices to students. Check at your school to see if this is a choice.

▶ **Homeowner's and renter's policies.** Homeowner's insurance is generally included in your mortgage payments, and you should be informed of its terms in the home purchasing process. Insurance is sometimes overlooked by renters, but it is a wise choice for protecting your belongings from theft and disasters such as fire. Insurance agencies typically offer some type of renter's insurance.

▶ **Vehicle insurance.** Automobile insurance includes several subcategories, including liability, collision, and comprehensive coverage. The amount and type of insurance that you purchase for your vehicle will depend on the age of your vehicle and the laws in your state. Know the types and amounts of coverage required by law in your location and, once again, shop for the best rates for the coverage that you are seeking.

apply it

Insurance Inventory and Research

GOAL: To become familiar with your insurance needs and make appropriate insurance choices.

STEP 1: Review the insurances that you currently have. Compare what you currently have to your needs and the insurance requirements in your state. Assess your insurances for their adequacy in meeting your needs and legal requirements.

STEP 2: Note any discrepancies that you find and create a brief plan to address them.

STEP 3: Research your options for correcting discrepancies according to your state guidelines and the suggestions in this chapter.

▶ REFLECTION QUESTIONS

- Have you ever been in a difficult situation related to a rental or major purchase?
- What were the circumstances that resulted in the difficulty?
- How was the difficulty resolved?

? CRITICAL THINKING QUESTIONS

7–7. What could you have done proactively that might have prevented the difficult situation?

7–8. What would you do differently in a future rental or major purchase situation?

7

▶ **Other insurance.** Other purchases might also warrant insurance. Items such as electronics and jewelry may require special policies or supplements (called riders) to your standard policy. It is often wise to insure items such as cell phones, PDAs, and laptop computers that are mobile and therefore more prone to loss and damage. Assess your situation and the items that you have and make wise decisions about your insurance policy.

PLANNING FINANCES BEYOND COLLEGE

As an adult student, there are considerations that you will need to make about your future beyond college. If you have family members for whom you are responsible, there are factors specific to their well-being that you will need to take into account.

This section of Chapter 7 provides an overview of future financial planning and investments. The purpose of this section is to introduce you to savings and investment and to future planning options, and to provide you with elements to consider. For specific advice and planning based on your individual circumstances, you should consult a personal financial advisor.

SAVING AND INVESTING

The AICPA (2004b) differentiates between saving and investing and concludes that both are important to financial planning. Saving typically includes accounts such as savings and checking accounts, certificates of deposit, and money markets. The value of these accounts remains fairly constant, and these accounts earn interest and dividends.

Investments are longer term and may increase or decrease in value over time. They may or may not pay interest or dividends. Typical investments include stocks, bonds, and mutual funds. Some of the important points related to investing that AICPA outlines include:

▶ **Ensure a sound financial foundation.** Make a thorough assessment of your financial status. Ensure that you have adequate reserve funds for emergencies and insurance coverage. Pay off significant credit card debt and have a realistic and workable budget before investing.

▶ **Use your employer's retirement plan benefits.** Employers typically offer opportunities to invest in retirement plans and may match funds that you invest into your plan. Take advantage of these types of funds offered by your employer. The human resources department typically provides information on these and other benefits.

▶ **Understand compounding over time.** Compounding occurs when the interest earned on an investment is reinvested into the principle and, in turn, earns additional interest. Consider the example from the AICPA of an initial investment of $1,000 that earns 8% annually. After a year, the total investment is worth $1,080.00 and will earn $86.40 in interest, resulting in a total of $1,166.40. The interest on this amount will be $93.31. In 9 years, the initial investment will be doubled, or worth $2,000.00, provided the interest rate remains constant. Investments compound significantly over time.

▶ **Consider the services of a financial planner.** There are many components to investing. Your individual situation and goals will help determine the amount of risk that you want to take in your investments, how accessible your earnings should be, and other relevant factors. A financial planner can also assist you in appropriate recordkeeping and provide advice on updating your investment portfolio. As a professional and expert, a financial planner will be able to help you consider all important aspects of investing.

TYPES OF INVESTMENTS

The U.S. Securities and Exchange Commission (SEC) identifies two major investment products: stocks and bonds, and mutual funds. Although there are variations on these, this chapter will address these two major categories as an introduction to investing. You are encouraged to research additional options and alternatives to these as you see appropriate to your situation.

Stocks and Bonds

When an investor purchases stock in a company, he or she is essentially "buying" a part of the company and becoming an "owner" that allows him or her a share of the earnings and profits proportionate to his or her investment. Stocks may earn more over time, but there is also greater potential for loss.

Bonds are an investment in the company as well, but the company uses the investment as a loan of sorts, paying it back to the investor over a designated amount of time with interest. Bonds are generally considered less of a risk than stocks, but may not provide as high a return (United States Security and Exchange Commission, 2004).

Mutual Funds

Professionals specializing in financial investments administer mutual funds. Their expertise lies in understanding various companies and selecting the best companies in which to invest. Individuals purchase shares in a fund of stocks and bonds from several selected companies. Earnings (and losses) reflect the earnings and losses of the entire fund. Because there are typically fees associated with mutual funds, it is important to assess the cost to ensure that the investment is worthwhile. Figure 7–2 defines several types of investments.

TYPES OF INVESTMENTS

Type of Investment	Explanation	General Parameters
Stocks	An investor becomes an "owner" of a company by purchasing stock in the company. The investor receives a share of the earnings and profits proportionate to his or her investment.	▶ May earn more on the initial investment. ▶ Greater potential for loss.
Bonds	A company uses investors' money as a loan, paying it back to the investor over a designated amount of time with interest.	▶ Generally less of a risk than stocks. ▶ May not provide as high a return on the initial investment.
Mutual Funds	Individuals purchase shares in a fund of stocks and bonds from several selected companies.	▶ Administered by professionals specializing in financial investments. ▶ Requires an understanding of the best companies in which to invest. ▶ Earnings and losses reflect the earnings and losses of the entire fund. ▶ There is usually a fee to cover administrative costs of mutual funds, so it is important to assess the costs.

FIGURE 7–2.   Various investments have different advantages and disadvantages. Know the benefits of each to make the wisest investments for your situation.

Adapted from United States Security and Exchange Commission (2004).

7

apply it

Banking and Investment Research

GOAL: *To become familiar with your banking and investment options and devise a banking and investment plan that is efficient and effective.*

STEP 1: Select several local banks that will be the focus of this activity.

STEP 2: Visit each bank or make an appointment with a personal banker.

STEP 3: Collect information regarding the types of accounts and investments that are available, as well as other services that the banks offer.

STEP 4: Determine wise choices for your own needs, based on the information that you gather.

ESTATE PLANNING

Proper planning of your estate (having a will) is critical if you have children. In any case, it is certainly wise to ensure that in the event of your death, your assets are distributed according to your wishes. Because of the legal aspects of estate planning and its individual nature, you should consult with the appropriate legal or financial professional for estate planning. Recognize the importance of completing this task thoroughly and updating the documentation regularly.

CHAPTER SUMMARY

The expenses associated with getting a college education in addition to the general cost of living can present challenges to students and their families. The goal of Chapter 7 was to review options for financing college and for managing personal finances as effectively as possible. In addition, you learned strategies for successfully completing major purchases and planning financially for your future.

Like the health considerations discussed in Chapter 6, sound financial management is a foundation for completing other life tasks. Having peace of mind about finances also significantly reduces stress. Consider as well that effective financial management while in school lays the groundwork for financial success in later years and will reflect positively on you in the future.

POINTS TO KEEP IN MIND

In this chapter, the following main points were discussed in detail:

- Financial considerations of college students should include personal finances, the wise use of credit, and creation of a realistic spending plan.
- It is important to build a strong credit history by establishing a credit history, but not abusing credit.
- Finances are an individualized and often complex matter. Seek the advice of a qualified financial advisor.
- A spending plan can determine your current spending patterns and lead you to make necessary adjustments to your budget.
- Online banking provides convenient and current access to your financial information.

7

▶ When renting or purchasing a house or apartment, know the local laws, understand your lease or loan terms, and be aware of your rights.

▶ When purchasing a home, seek the services of a qualified real estate professional and home inspector.

▶ Know the legalities and agreement terms regarding any major product or insurance purchase.

▶ Know the types of insurance that are available and what each covers.

▶ Carefully research financial aid options and apply by completing the FAFSA. Many students qualify for aid because of the many factors that are considered.

▶ Complete financial aid forms thoroughly and carefully. Check them for errors and keep copies.

▶ Types of financial aid include loans, grants, scholarships, and work-study. The type for which you might qualify depends on numerous individual factors.

▶ Understand your banking and investment options in order to maximize the effectiveness of your financial planning.

LEARNING OBJECTIVES REVISITED

Review the learning objectives for this chapter and rate your level of achievement for each objective using the rating scale provided. For each objective on which you do not rate yourself as a 3, outline a plan of action that you will take to fully achieve the objective. Include a time frame for this plan.

1 = did not successfully achieve objective

2 = understand what is needed, but need more study or practice

3 = achieved learning objective thoroughly

	1	2	3
Describe general financial considerations that must be made during college attendance.	☐	☐	☐
Discuss management of credit.	☐	☐	☐
Discuss elements to consider when making major purchases.	☐	☐	☐
Define various forms of financial assistance and locate resources for each.	☐	☐	☐
Be able to determine a workable budget based on recommended budgeting principles.	☐	☐	☐
Explain basic financial investments and the advantages and disadvantages of each.	☐	☐	☐

Steps to Achieve Unmet Objectives

Steps   Due Date

1. _____   _____

2. _____   _____

3. _____   _____

4. _____   _____

SUGGESTED ITEMS FOR LEARNING PORTFOLIO

▶ Creating a Spending Plan: Add this to your portfolio as a baseline and guide to use in future budgeting.

▶ Budgeting Resources on the Web: The purpose of this activity is to compile a list of resources available on the Internet.

▶ Banking and Investment Research: Compiling this information will allow you to make wise banking and investment choices as your financial needs change.

▶ Credit Research: You can use the list of guidelines you compile about using credit as a checklist to monitor your own credit habits and make changes as necessary.

▶ Insurance Inventory and Research: Use this inventory and related resources as a method for assessing and monitoring your insurance needs and updating your insurance coverages as needed.

7

REFERENCES

American Institute of Certified Public Accountants. (2004a). Personal financial planning: Budgeting and saving. Retrieved March 4, 2005, from http://pfp.aicpa.org/Resources/Consumer+Content/Learn+More+About+Personal+Financial+Planning/

American Institute of Certified Public Accountants. (2004b). Investment planning—the basics. Retrieved March 4, 2005, from http://www.360financialliteracy.org/Financial+Topics/Investment+Planning/

California State University–Sacramento. (n.d.). Subsidized vs. unsubsidized loans. Retrieved August 25, 2005, from http://www.csus.edu/sfsc-ymm/03_student_loans/sub_and_unsub.html

CollegeData.com (2004a). What is financial aid? A service of First Financial Bank. Retrieved February 24, 2005, from http://www.collegedata.com/cs/content/content_payarticle_tmpl.jhtml?articleId=10075

CollegeData.com (2004b). It starts with financial need. A service of First Financial Bank. Retrieved February 24, 2005, from http://www.collegedata.com/cs/content/content_payarticle_tmpl.jhtml?articleId=10079

CollegeData.com (2004c). Tips for your financial aid forms. A service of First Financial Bank. Retrieved February 24, 2005, from http://www.collegedata.com/cs/content/content_payarticle_tmpl.jhtml?articleId=10091

Duguay, D. (2003). Develop a credit history during college. Excerpt from Duguay, D., *Don't Spend Your Raise.* New York: McGraw-Hill. Retrieved February 25, 2005, from the Young Money Web site: http://www.youngmoney.com/credit_debt/credit_basics/021107_01

Schmidgall, W. (2002). Group warns students of pitfalls of credit card debts. *The Daily Vidette,* Illinois State University. Retrieved February 25, 2005, from the Young Money Web site: http://www.youngmoney.com/credit_debt/credit_basics/021007_05

United States Department of Education. (2006). Federal student aid at a glance. *Funding Education beyond High School: The Guide to Federal Student Aid.* Retrieved May 1, 2006, from http://studentaid.ed.gov/students/publications/student_guide/2006-2007/index.html

United States Department of Education. (n.d.). Looking for student aid: Federal, state, and other sources of information. Retrieved March 4, 2005, from http://studentaid.ed.gov/students/attachments/siteresources/LSA.pdf

United States Department of Housing and Urban Development. (2003). Don't be a victim of loan fraud. Retrieved March 5, 2005, from http://www.hud.gov/offices/hsg/sfh/buying/loanfraud.cfm

United States Department of Housing and Urban Development. (2005). Common questions from first-time home buyers. Retrieved May 1, 2006, from http://www.hud.gov/buying/comq.cfm

United States Securities and Exchange Commission. (2004). Investment products: Your choices. Retrieved March 4, 2005, from http://www.sec.gov/investor/pubs/roadmap/choice.htm

7

Young Money. (2002a). Financial basics for college students. Retrieved February 24, 2005, from http://www.youngmoney.com/credit_debt/credit_basics/020809_02

Young Money. (2002b). Putting a spending plan together. Retrieved February 24, 2005, from http://www.youngmoney.com/money_management/budgeting/020809_06

7

© BananaStock Ltd.

CHAPTER OUTLINE

8 Information Literacy for the Twenty-First Century

THE BIG PICTURE

LEARNING OBJECTIVES

By the end of this chapter, you will achieve the following objectives:

▶ Define *information literacy* and explain the necessity for developing these skills for academic and career success.

▶ Describe common library resources and explain their use in finding school- and career-related information.

▶ Demonstrate the ability to use Internet resources effectively in research.

▶ Demonstrate the ability to assess the credibility of information sources.

▶ Define *copyright* and *plagiarism* and demonstrate the ability to avoid plagiarism and cite resources correctly.

TOPIC SCENARIO

Anita Franklin recently graduated with an Associate degree in Network Administration. She was quickly hired as an assistant network administrator for a medium-size company and has the responsibility for maintaining about 25 computers networked to a main server, as well as several laptop computers used by mobile employees in the field. Tasks in her job description include answering computer user questions and solving computer problems for the company's employees, keeping software and security tools current on employee machines, and researching and providing input into the purchase of new technology tools, including those for general business tasks, communication, and meeting the needs of specialized departments. When new tools are acquired and implemented, Anita also must help teach employees how to use the tools accurately and efficiently. Based on this short description of Anita's job, answer the following questions:

▶ Think forward to the job position you are seeking as a result of your academic training. How do Anita's challenges relate to what you foresee in your own career?

▶ What information challenges do you think Anita is faced with on a daily basis?

▶ Compared to what Anita learned in school, what information do you think has changed since graduation or will be changing soon?

▶ What knowledge and skills do you think Anita must continue to acquire to order to advance in her job and career? Where might Anita get this information?

▶ How will Anita know she has the most accurate and up-to-date information possible?

8

INFORMATION LITERACY IN THE TWENTY-FIRST CENTURY: AN OVERVIEW

In the age of enormous amounts of quickly changing information, students and professionals alike must be able to find information and put it to use effectively. Students must be able to access information beyond textbooks and classroom instructors in order to prepare for the workplace. Professionals must keep current and continuously expand their body of knowledge to be successful and to advance in their careers. Staying successfully updated requires individuals to be *information literate*.

Traditional libraries offer many sources of information. Many libraries have provided access to their resources via the Internet, providing their library patrons with added convenience. Apart from libraries, the Internet also opens the door to a wealth of additional resources. Entire courses can be devoted to information literacy; however, this chapter focuses only on basic and essential skills for students and provides a foundation for more advanced information skills ultimately needed for workplace success. Excellent students will pursue these basic topics more fully, practice these skills in each course they take, and relate the concepts specifically to their field of study and career goals using the resources and suggestions provided here.

WHAT IS INFORMATION LITERACY?

According to the American Library Association's competency standards for information literacy (2004), an information-literate person is "able to recognize when information is needed and has the ability to locate, evaluate, and use the information effectively." Information-literate individuals are necessarily computer literate, library literate, and technology literate, meaning that they can effectively use the computer, library, and the Internet and other technologies to efficiently access information. Information-literate individuals are also able to critically assess information and to use it effectively to solve personal and workplace problems.

THE TWENTY-FIRST CENTURY LEARNER RESPONSIBILITY

New ideas, technologies, processes, and other essential information are added to the body of knowledge on a daily basis. Students and professionals alike must take on the responsibility for becoming competent learners and then continue learning throughout their careers. If students in academic institutions rely solely on the information that they gain from textbooks or from instructors, without developing effective learning skills themselves, they will be at a significant disadvantage in the workplace. Summarizing the American Library Association standards for information literacy for students in higher education (2004), an information-literate student should be able to

▶ determine what kind and how much information is needed.

▶ access information effectively and efficiently.

▶ evaluate information critically.

▶ use information effectively to accomplish a specific goal individually or as a member of a group.

▶ use information ethically and legally.

8

REFLECTION QUESTIONS

• How effectively are you able to find information in a library?

• What is your level of skill in using the computer and Internet for finding and using information?

? CRITICAL THINKING QUESTIONS

8–1. What is your reaction to the following statement? "If it is published in writing or on the Internet, it is probably true."

8–2. What specific questions do you ask to distinguish between good information and questionable information?

ADVANTAGES OF BEING INFORMATION LITERATE

When learners become information literate, they increase their advantages in school and in the workplace. The following list represents just a few of these potential advantages:

> Learners sharpen their critical and creative thinking skills.

> Learners develop higher-order thinking skills essential for excellence in school and the workplace.

> Students develop a deeper and more applicable understanding of the content they are learning and become better prepared for their jobs.

> Individuals are able to communicate in knowledgeable, logical, and defensible ways regarding their work.

> The ability to effectively participate in problem solving and decision making is enhanced.

> Professionals are able to keep up with advancements in their field of study, making them more competent and valuable as employees.

Using the library and understanding the resources that are available to you as a student will contribute greatly to your success in college.

LIBRARY RESOURCES: THE BASICS

Information-literate individuals can figure out the organization of the library facilities they visit. They are also able to identify the various resources available and understand how to use these resources effectively. This knowledge provides an important foundation for using an effective search strategy to find the answers to questions or to solve workplace problems. Understanding the resources allows the researcher to know where to most effectively start the search process. Library resources include a variety of reference tools, sources of current and archived information, and other media sources beyond the printed format.

REFERENCE RESOURCES

There are numerous reference resources available in most libraries. Information-literate individuals should understand the information found in each resource as well as how to use the resources efficiently to answer questions.

Dictionaries and Thesauruses

A dictionary is an alphabetical listing of words. Typically, dictionaries also show how to pronounce the words, give variations on spelling and word forms, and provide the different meanings and uses of the word. Though a general dictionary is sufficient for basic writing tasks, information-literate individuals should be aware that technical and discipline-specific words are not always found in general dictionaries. The information provided in subject-specific dictionaries is typically more detailed and similar to that found in an encyclopedia. Subject-specific dictionaries often include illustrations and other reference information. Examples of subject-specific dictionaries include medical dictionaries, computer user or technical dictionaries, electronics dictionaries, slang dictionaries, and so forth. There are numerous subject-specific dictionaries available.

A thesaurus is book of synonyms. It can also include antonyms (opposite words) and phrases or slang terms for words. As with subject-specific dictionaries, specialized thesauruses can include specialized expressions for a particular field such as medicine or computer science.

Encyclopedias, Almanacs, Handbooks, and Atlases

An encyclopedia is a collection of detailed articles on a wide range of subjects. Encyclopedias can be either general (e.g., *World Book Encyclopedia*) or subject specific (e.g., *Encyclopedia of Psychology*), just as with dictionaries and thesauruses. Subject-specific encyclopedias contain more detailed articles related to specific fields and are written by experts in that field.

An almanac provides up-to-date figures, charts, tables, statistics, and other information. Almanac producers usually publish a revised edition each year. Almanacs can be found for almost any subject (i.e., sports, countries, history, religion, etc.) and are excellent sources for current facts and statistics.

A handbook provides very concise data, usually in table or chart form, on specialized subject areas (e.g., electronics, human resources, adverse drug interactions, etc.). A handbook is an excellent reference for current statistics, procedures, instructions, or specific reference information on specific topics.

An atlas is generally thought of as a collection of maps; however, atlases can also be a collection of other visual information, such as those used in the study of anatomy. They can also provide a wealth of supplemental information in text, charts, or tables related to the illustrations. As with other reference tools, atlases can be very subject specific, as in historical atlases, anatomical atlases, or political atlases.

Periodicals

A periodical is a collection of articles and other information published at regular intervals such as daily, weekly, monthly, or bimonthly. The focus of each periodical is very specific to a topic area, location, viewpoint, or treatment of the material. Newspapers, popular magazines, trade journals, and scholarly journals are examples of periodicals. Information-literate individuals understand the different purposes of each type of periodical and the kinds of information each provides.

Newspapers are periodicals that provide very current information, including news, stories, and commentaries. Most newspapers concentrate on a specific geographic area. Although most journalists and editors take care to present accurate information, newspapers can be biased toward a specific viewpoint and can include information that is skewed according to a particular perspective.

Popular magazines, scholarly journals, and trade journals are periodicals that are often confused. Popular magazines (e.g., *TIME, Glamour, Business Week*) are written for the general public and typically have shorter articles written by journalists. The articles are not usually evaluated by experts in the field and they typically do not include a reference list (a listing of the sources of information) so that readers can check the facts themselves. Popular magazines are filled with advertising, can be biased toward a specific viewpoint, and can contain inaccuracies.

On the other hand, scholarly journals are periodicals written for very specific audiences and typically include longer articles written by subject matter experts using the jargon or specialized terminology of a certain field. Scholarly journals (e.g., *Journal of the American Medical Association*) commonly use a very structured format for their articles, which typically include an abstract (concise overview), introduction, literature review of background information, methodology, results, conclusion, and bibliography. Articles in scholarly journals are generally critically evaluated by experts from the field to ensure that the facts, statements, and conclusions are as accurate as possible. When experts evaluate the articles in a journal, it is called a *refereed* journal. Scholarly journals have minimal advertising, strive to be nonbiased, and take many steps to ensure the accuracy of information. Scholarly journals report original research and describe research programs, procedures, theories, and concepts.

Trade journals are periodicals that lie somewhere in between popular magazines and scholarly journals in terms of types of articles, authorship, and steps taken to avoid bias and ensure accuracy. Trade journals (e.g., *Pharmaceutical Processing Magazine*) are written especially for industry professionals in a very specific field. They provide product information and articles on current trends and practices. Trade journals contain advertising very specific to the journal's audience. Though care is taken to avoid bias and to ensure accuracy, these journals are often not as strict as refereed journals.

Databases and Directories

A database is a collection of data organized so that a user can easily access the information. Many different databases are accessible from libraries and from the Internet. Examples include indexes, catalogs, and other kinds of

apply it

Journal Analysis

GOAL: *To help develop an understanding of the differences between scholarly journals and popular magazines.*

STEP 1: Find a refereed journal for an area in your field of study. Go to the journal's Web site and read the author guidelines.

STEP 2: In the same journal, find a research article of interest and read the article.

STEP 3: In groups of four or five students, compare the article with the author guidelines. How closely do you think the author met the guidelines? Is there anything you especially liked about the article? Is there anything you found to be confusing, invalid, ambiguous, or otherwise problematic? Write a brief analysis.

STEP 4: Answer the following questions about the articles this journal will accept: Is there more than one kind of article that the journal will accept? Is there a length maximum and/or minimum requirement? By whom will the article be reviewed?

STEP 5: Now use a periodical index to find an article in a popular magazine.

STEP 6: Answer the following questions: How is the format of the magazine article different from that of the journal article? Do the magazine articles appear to follow a similar structured format like those in the journal? Can you find author guidelines for this magazine? What other differences are there between the two types of periodicals?

STEP 7: Consider putting this Journal Analysis project in your Learning Portfolio.

8

databases in both print and electronic formats. Databases help researchers find additional sources of information.

A directory is similar to a database except that the data is typically an organized listing of information such as names, addresses, phone numbers, members, associations, and so forth, arranged alphabetically or by category. Directories are available in both print and electronic formats.

Librarians have access to literally hundreds of databases and directories for all kinds of information. Electronic formats allow convenient searching of the resource using techniques that narrow the focus of the search to pinpoint the exact data needed. Information-literate individuals have developed skill in using these resources to find information.

Multimedia

Information can be in a form other than print or electronic. Many libraries house or have access to a variety of graphic, audio, video, and film media sources of information that researchers may find useful. Examples include maps, videotapes, CD-ROMs, DVDs, 16-mm films, audiotapes, and so forth. Each library or library system has access to different media or can often borrow a desired media resource from another library using interlibrary loan.

apply it

Resource Listing

GOAL: *To develop an organized list of resources that will be useful for work and career research activities.*

STEP 1: Define each of the following library resources and briefly explain its purpose: dictionaries (general and subject specific), encyclopedias (general and subject specific), directories, newspapers, popular magazines, scholarly and trade journals, periodical indexes, professional or trade organizations, search engines, online libraries, and Web portals.

STEP 2: Then give at least two examples of specific resources under each category that apply to your field of study. Include both physical library and online versions of the resources.

STEP 3: Consider using this list as a starting point for the Resource List in your Learning Portfolio.

LIBRARY ORGANIZATION

Libraries must use some kind of catalog system to describe the items they have available and to tell where these items are located physically in the library. Libraries organize their materials by subject matter (called cataloging), meaning that materials on the same topic can be found together in the library. In order to find out where an item is located, two tools are necessary: (1) a way to access the catalog and (2) an address for the item, called a call number.

There are two main classification systems that libraries in the English-speaking world use to organize their materials: the Library of Congress Classification and the Dewey Decimal System. It is important to identify which system a library uses in order to efficiently look for materials in that library. Within each system, items on the same topic are grouped together and assigned a number or set of letters and numbers so that the item can be identified uniquely.

8

The Library of Congress Classification

The Library of Congress (LC; our national library) has defined the terms and phrases to help organize library materials in a way that is consistent across the nation. These terms and phrases are called subject headings. Subject headings are further divided into more precise headings called sub-headings. A library item may have multiple subject headings if the item deals with more than one major topic. Subject headings are useful when conducting electronic searches. The official *Library of Congress Subject Headings (LCSH)* publication is a listing of the subject headings and is published in several volumes, usually found in the reference area of a library. The front pages of the first volume of the *LCSH* describe specifically how to use this system. Librarians are also very knowledgeable in its use. Not only does the *LCSH* describe the categorization of a library's resources, but many libraries also use this system to physically organize their resources in the library itself. The Library of Congress Classification uses 21 main classes identified by letters, which are broken down into subdivisions noted by an additional letter or two, in some cases. These subdivisions are further divided into very specific sections noted by numbers. See Figure 8–1 for an example.

DIAGRAM OF LC SYSTEM CATEGORIES

Library of Congress Subject Heading Categories

A – General Works	M – Music and Books on Music
B – Philosophy, Psychology, Religion	N – Fine Arts
C – Auxiliary Sciences of History	P – Language and Literature
D – History (general) and History of Europe	Q – Science
E – History: America	R – Medicine
F – History: America	S – Agriculture
G – Geography, Anthropology, Recreation	T – Technology
H – Social Sciences	U – Military Science
J – Political Science	V – Naval Science
K – Law	Z – Bibliography, Library Science, Information Resources (general)
L – Education	

FIGURE 8–1. The Library of Congress subject headings are one classification system for library resources.

The Dewey Decimal System

The Dewey Decimal Classification (DDC) is another classification system used to organize materials within the library. As with the Library of Congress system, like topics are grouped together in numbered categories, in this case ranging from 000 to 900. These ten categories are then further divided into progressively more precise subdivisions using whole and decimal numbers, starting with the main class number (OCLC, 2003, p. 7). Figure 8–2 shows the major categories of the DDC. Many libraries use this system to identify their resources and to physically organize their resources instead of the LC system.

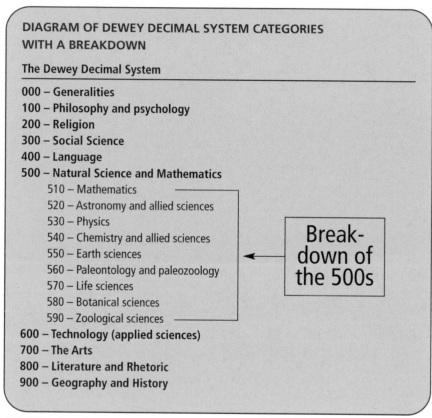

DIAGRAM OF DEWEY DECIMAL SYSTEM CATEGORIES WITH A BREAKDOWN

The Dewey Decimal System

000 – Generalities
100 – Philosophy and psychology
200 – Religion
300 – Social Science
400 – Language
500 – Natural Science and Mathematics
    510 – Mathematics
    520 – Astronomy and allied sciences
    530 – Physics
    540 – Chemistry and allied sciences
    550 – Earth sciences
    560 – Paleontology and paleozoology
    570 – Life sciences
    580 – Botanical sciences
    590 – Zoological sciences
600 – Technology (applied sciences)
700 – The Arts
800 – Literature and Rhetoric
900 – Geography and History

Break-down of the 500s

FIGURE 8–2.   The Dewey Decimal System is the classification system of library resources used by most public libraries.

The Call Number

Most libraries label each library item with a call number that provides sufficient information to locate the item. A call number is like a library item's address, telling the researcher exactly where the item is located in a particular library. The call number is found on a label on the spine or outside front cover (for small items) of the item. By understanding the call number and the specific classification system being used at that library, a researcher should be able to go to the exact location of the item in the library. See examples of call numbers for the two classification system in Figures 8–3 and 8–4.

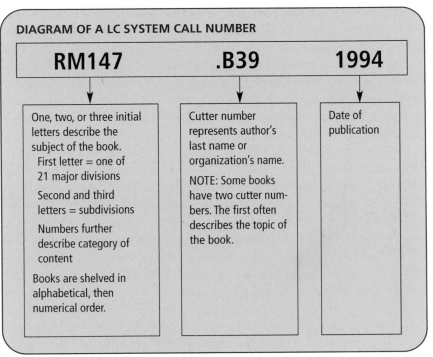

FIGURE 8–3. Understanding the Library of Congress Classification call number will help you locate materials organized using this method.

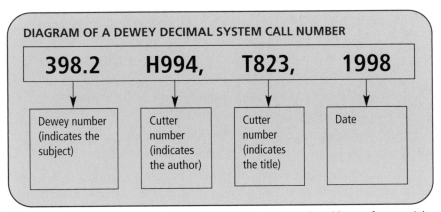

FIGURE 8–4. The Dewey Decimal System uses call numbers as the addresses for materials on the library shelves.

Catalogs and Indexes

To find the call number and other information about items in a library, a researcher must go to a library catalog. A catalog provides a record of every item found in a specific library. Most libraries are automated, meaning that their catalogs are electronically accessible via a computer or on the Internet.

A few smaller libraries may still have card catalogs, which are printed cards in physical file cabinets at the library location. The information on this catalog record includes the call number, the author, title, edition, publisher, a brief physical description of the item, notes about the item's content, and valid Library of Congress subject headings assigned to the item. Most, electronic catalogs allow for searching by author, title, subject heading (valid assigned LC subject headings), and keywords (related words, but not necessarily valid LC subject headings).

Library catalogs do not include articles found in periodicals. To find a specific article, a periodical index is required. A periodical index provides reference to articles in a specific set of periodicals, usually for a specific range of dates. An important difference between a library's catalog and a periodical index is that a periodical index does not reflect the periodicals held in a specific library. Periodical indexes are published by commercial entities and index a pre-established set of periodicals whether or not a specific library subscribes to all of the periodicals referenced in the index. Once a researcher finds an article of interest in a periodical, the next step is to determine if that library actually subscribes to the specific periodical and has the issue needed. If so, the researcher can physically go to the periodical and read the article. Typically, periodicals cannot be checked out of the library; however, a photocopy of the article can be made. If the library does not subscribe to the desired periodical, the researcher has three options:

1. Find a library that does subscribe to the periodical and go physically to read or copy the article. Follow legal and ethical guidelines for making copies. Generally, one copy for educational use is permitted. Read the publication's copyright guidelines before making any copies.

2. Request that a copy of the article be sent to the home library, which usually incurs a fee per page.

3. Access the article electronically using a full-text resource, available either through the library or on the Internet.

There are thousands of periodical indexes, covering over 150,000 individual periodicals. The first step in using a periodical index is to determine which periodicals the index covers and for what period of time. As with most other library reference materials, there are general periodical indexes and subject-specific periodical indexes. General indexes cover a broad range of topics in scholarly journals, popular magazines, and newspapers. Subject-specific periodical indexes cover articles in selected scholarly journals related to a broad topic area (e.g., *Business Periodicals Index* and *Index to Legal Periodicals*). To choose the most appropriate periodical index, it is best to consult a librarian.

All periodical indexes provide the same type of information, even though they may be formatted differently. The information provided includes the title of the periodical, the date of the issue that contains the article, the volume number and page numbers of the article, the title of the article, a few words or phrases about the article content, the author(s), the abstract, and the subject headings.

success steps

STEPS FOR USING A PERIODICAL INDEX

Step 1: Develop a list of keywords and subject headings for your topic.

Step 2: Determine the specific periodical index to use (one for scholarly journals, magazines, newspapers, or a particular subject), using these guidelines:

   a. Periodicals (not articles in periodicals) are listed in the library's catalog.

   b. Ask a librarian for assistance!

Step 3: Use the search word list and the periodical index to find the exact citation for the article(s) you want to read.

   a. Read the introductory material in a printed periodical index to see detailed instructions.

   b. Use the search tool in an electronic index.

Step 4: Go to the location in the library for the periodicals and use the periodical, volume, and page number to find the article.

   a. In larger libraries, periodicals are often stored separately depending on if they are current (recently received) or bound (copies that are bound into books, typically by volumes).

   b. Older periodicals may be in a different place entirely, such as the basement.

REFLECTION QUESTIONS

- What library resources do you typically use when conducting research for school? Which resources discussed here do you think you will find useful and why?
- In order of importance and usefulness to you as a student, how would you rate the resources discussed here? Why?

CRITICAL THINKING QUESTIONS

8–3. How might advertisements affect the credibility of the different types of periodicals?

8–4. What sources of bias can be present in articles in periodicals?

apply it

Visit the Library

GOAL: *To become oriented to the library or libraries that will be used most during school.*

STEP 1: Go physically to your school and your local libraries and review the different resources discussed in this chapter. Consider participating in an organized library tour typically offered for patrons.

STEP 2: Make or collect a map, listing, and description of the resources available and the location of those resources.

8

THE INTERNET: BROADENING THE RESOURCE POOL

The Internet has made researching easier by providing access to a wide variety of information. In addition, the Internet facilitates searching for information with search engines, online reference resources, online indexes and directories, and entire virtual libraries.

BASIC TOOLS ON THE INTERNET

Since there are millions of Internet sites, it is essential to have an efficient way of searching. Two important tools for searching the Internet efficiently are search engines and subject directories. Understanding these tools is essential to using effective search strategies to find information efficiently.

Search Engines and Subject Directories

Search engines are tools that facilitate searching on the Internet. Basically, they are a collection of Internet files (not all the files on the Internet, however) that allow an Internet user to search through the files using keywords and a search engine mechanism. There are many different search engines on the Internet that can be used to find information. However, since each search engine allows searching through only those Internet files in its particular database, using only one search engine supplies only a small portion of the available sites on the Internet. To find a more complete list of Web sites and Internet files, multiple search engines should be used. Google is a well-known example of a search engine with a large database. Search engines are good for general information.

Subject directories are excellent tools for research-oriented searches or when you want to find sites recommended by experts. A subject directory is a collection of links to a large number of Internet resources. Typically the links are organized by topic area. There are two types of subject directories. Commercial directories are general in nature and are less selective in the links they provide. Academic and professional directories are usually maintained by experts and cater to professionals needing credible information. These directories are excellent research tools for highly specialized information. INFOMINE, The Internet Public Library, and Librarians' Index to the Internet are excellent examples of professional subject directories.

Electronic Searching Techniques

There are some basic techniques that can help focus or expand a search using an electronic search tool. To define your search terms more precisely,

8

! RESOURCE BOX

EXAMPLES OF ELECTRONIC SEARCH ENGINES AND SUBJECT DIRECTORIES
- Google
- Teoma
- Yahoo!
- INFOMINE
- The Internet Public Library
- Librarians' Index to the Internet

use Boolean operators such as AND, OR, and NOT. The operator AND is used to retrieve results where *all* the words separated by AND are included. The operator OR is used to retrieve results where either of the words separated by OR are included. Finally, the operator NOT is used to retrieve results where the word preceded by NOT is excluded. Implied Boolean operators include using a plus sign (+) in front of a word to retrieve results that include the word and a minus (–) in front of a word to retrieve results that exclude the word, similar to the AND and NOT operators. Quotation marks around phrases are used to retrieve results where that specific phrase is included. Most search tools have an "Advanced Search" link that provides a form to help focus or narrow the searches. These advanced search tips and tools explain the search language used by that search tool.

success steps

STEPS FOR EXPLORING THE USE OF BOOLEAN OPERATORS

1. Select a topic you would like to research. The topic should be identified by a phrase. "MyPyramid" is an example.

2. Experiment with the various Boolean operators, both in words and symbols. For example, use "food guide +pyramid"; then try "food guide not pyramid" and "food guide or pyramid" and compare your results.

3. Try other searches specific to your field. Experiment with various combinations of search terms and operators to gain an understanding of the types of results you obtain.

4. Note your observations regarding the results you obtain using different operators in your searches. Note which results would be most useful in various situations.

RESOURCES AVAILABLE ON THE INTERNET

Many of the resources available in a physical library are now available on the Internet via virtual libraries, subject directories, and individual Web sites. There are numerous free and fee-based sites that provide information-literate users with valuable resources at their fingertips.

Online Reference Resources

Reference resources such as dictionaries, thesauruses, encyclopedias, almanacs, handbooks, and directories can be accessed online via the Internet.

8

! RESOURCE BOX

EXAMPLES OF REFERENCE WEB SITES
- Refdesk.com
- Questia.com
- Merriam-Webster Online
- Grove Art Online
- Encyclopedia.com
- Occupational Outlook Handbook

Hundreds of both general and subject-specific resources are available, covering almost every industry. Though some Web sites require registration and sometimes a monthly or annual access fee, many sites are free. A few sites allow free use of basic services while charging a fee for more advanced or expanded services. One of the most important benefits of accessing these resources using the Internet is the ability to use search tools to locate the specific information needed.

Online Periodicals

As mentioned earlier, if your library does not subscribe to a desired periodical, one of the options is to find a full-text version of the article online. The general procedure for searching for online full-text articles is basically the same as in a physical library. An online periodical index is used to find the needed information. In many cases, the actual full-text article can be viewed online either for free or for a fee. Many online libraries and subject directories also link to periodical indexes and the articles themselves.

Web Portals

A Web portal (sometimes called a gateway) is a Web site that provides links to many different kinds of information, either for a general audience or related to a specific interest group or industry. Web portals are useful in finding industry-related information, products, news, periodicals, organizations, chat rooms, people's addresses or phone numbers, and almost anything else related to the industry that can be found on the Internet. Some Web portals are maintained by ISPs (Internet service providers, such as AOL and Yahoo!), while others are maintained by state governments, professional organizations, or some other special interest entity. There are hundreds of Web portals for almost any industry or interest group on the Internet. Note that some Web portals are commercial in nature but can still provide useful resources.

Professional and Trade Organizations

Professional and trade organizations include members with similar interests or occupations. These organizations are excellent sources for current information about an industry, for trends and current practices, for licensure and certification requirements, and for networking with professionals. Most organizations have some kind of online presence and many provide excellent information on their home pages. Students and professionals can keep

---

RESOURCE BOX

EXAMPLES OF PERIODICAL INDEX WEB SITES
- PubMed Central
- HighBeam
- NewsLink
- FindArticles

RESOURCE BOX

WEB PORTALS
- AOL
- About
- Forbes
- FirstGov

RESOURCE BOX

FIND EXAMPLES OF OTHER PROFESSIONAL ORGANIZATION SITES ON THE WEB, SUCH AS:
- Information Technology Association of America (ITAA)
- The Computer Technology Industry Association (CompTIA)
- American Health Information Management Association (AHIMA)
- American Association of Medical Assistants (AAMA)
- National Cosmetology Association (NCA)

8

current in their field by participating in a professional organization's activities and learning about current issues. A good starting place to find appropriate professional organization Web sites is the Google Directory listing for professional organizations.

CONDUCTING RESEARCH: STRATEGIES AND ISSUES

Knowing the tools available and how to use the tools to find information are only two of the information literacy skills. An important third element is knowing how to determine what information is needed and to develop an effective and efficient plan of action for the search. Once information is found, the person who is information literate knows what to do with this information, including how to communicate it to others.

MAKING A PLAN FOR RESEARCH

Good research starts with a plan of action. Being information literate includes the ability to develop a good research plan and use library and online resources effectively and efficiently, avoid unproductive searching, and understand when and where to get help. As with solving any problem, the first step is to understand specifically the task at hand and the parameters within which the task must be completed.

RESEARCH ETHICS AND LEGALITIES

Information-literate individuals understand the legal and ethical ramifications of accessing and using information. Important concepts to understand include plagiarism, copyright, and appropriate methods for citing other people's work.

Plagiarism and Copyright

Review the discussion of plagiarism in chapter 5. Recall that plagiarism is copying and presenting someone else's work as your own without giving him or her appropriate credit. Copyright is the legal right of ownership to the work.

The advancement of the Internet and technology in general has made it easier to plagiarize the works of others due to the accessibility of information. Important considerations for using information include

REFLECTION QUESTIONS

- What steps do you currently take to find information on the Internet? Write the steps down, analyze them, and see if you can make the process more efficient.
- What professional organizations are appropriate for you in your field of study? How can you get involved today?

? CRITICAL THINKING QUESTIONS

8–5. How do online search engines work? How might the way a search engine operates affect the results of a search?

8–6. How do online subject directories work? How are subject directories different from search engines? (This may take some research!)

8

The Internet is an ever-expanding source of research and reference material, including directories, professional organizations, and other resources.

STEPS FOR STARTING THE RESEARCH PROCESS

Step 1:   Clearly identify the task. If researching for a specific project, be sure to read your project instructions carefully or ask enough questions to understand exactly what the project requires. What is your task? How long does your project need to be? How current does your information need to be? What kinds of resources should you use? Are there a specific number of resources required? For what audience are you writing?

Step 2:   Develop the topic in detail. A good start to developing a topic is to frame the task in the form of a question. Next, brainstorm a list of additional questions that could be asked to answer the main question. In the brainstorming phase, do not evaluate or judge the questions, just list them. Then, review the question list and develop the topic more fully. If necessary, read about the topic in an encyclopedia or another broadly focused resource to make sure the background has been reviewed sufficiently.

Step 3:   Create an outline of major topics and subtopics. This strategy works well even for minor research tasks. In some cases, the initial questions and outline may change as you find more information.

Step 4:   Generate a list of keywords and phrases and subject headings. Organize keywords appropriately to produce a useful list. Refine your search phrases to broaden or narrow the focus as needed. Remember to include the official Library of Congress subject headings in your list. Add to this list as the search continues.

Step 5:   Conduct the search using the library or online catalogs and indexes. Follow the appropriate procedures for each tool. Ask the librarian for ideas or help as needed. Write down the entire call number, title, and author of resources for future reference.

Step 6:   Locate the actual resource either in the library or online. Review the bibliography of the resources you find to continue finding additional items. Continue revising your search term list and outline as needed.

8

avoiding plagiarism and correctly documenting or citing information sources to give credit where credit is due. It is important to apply the concepts regarding plagiarism that were covered in chapter 5 of this text. Plagiarism guidelines apply to all information, regardless of the source.

EVALUATING ONLINE INFORMATION

Once information is found, it must be evaluated to determine if it is appropriate, credible, and current. Anyone can put information on the Internet and can do so for a multitude of reasons. No individual or organization edits, controls, or verifies the information on the Internet; therefore, Internet users must view information they find very critically. At a minimum, researchers should ask the following questions about the Web site from which they are getting information, in order to determine the value of the information they find:

▶ **Sponsorship.** Who or what organization sponsors the Web site and what are their motives for doing so? Are they trying to inform, sell something, or persuade the reader to agree to a specific way of thinking? Is there some other motive? What does the URL (uniform resource locator) tell you? Look at the ending of the URL to determine if the site is an educational site (.edu), a commercial site (.com), a government site (.gov), and so forth. Is the site from a foreign country? (A foreign country's Web site does not mean that the information is not valid, but the information might not apply to the laws or policies of the United States.) Is the site hosted by an ISP such as MSN or an agency or organization? What does the "About Us" or other information say about the sponsorship and purpose of the site?

▶ **Authorship.** Who authored the content and are they qualified to do so? What are their credentials? Are they associated with an organization that lends more credibility to their statements, such as a government agency or academic institution?

▶ **Currency.** Is the information dated, revised regularly, and current? Are original and revision dates on the site? Are the cited resources current?

▶ **Quality of information.** Does the information appear to be of high quality? Does it agree with other sources of information you have read? Is it logical? Do the links to other sites work and are these sites credible? Are statements supported with references to other works, as might be found in a scholarly journal? Can you actually find these references? Are permissions to reproduce someone else's

▶ REFLECTION QUESTIONS

- Do you think you ever plagiarize in your schoolwork? If so, how?
- What specific steps can you take to avoid this practice?

8

CRITICAL THINKING QUESTIONS

8–7. What kind of questions should be asked about printed products found in a library?

8–8. How is the credibility of information found in a library different from that found online?

8–9. What citation style is most often used in your industry?

information noted? Can the resources be found in a traditional library?

▶ **Objectivity.** Is the site biased toward a specific viewpoint? If so, does the site state that the information is a viewpoint or does it present the viewpoint as fact? Are all viewpoints addressed or just one perspective?

apply it

Web Site Evaluation

GOAL: *To develop a checklist for evaluating Web sites.*

STEP 1: Develop a checklist you can use for assessing any Web site using the criteria discussed in this chapter.

STEP 2: Find one Web site that you consider to be of high credibility and one site that you consider to be of low credibility.

STEP 3: As a group, write a brief explanation addressing each criterion, explaining how the site meets or does not meet the criteria.

STEP 4: Consider placing this worksheet in your Learning Portfolio.

CHAPTER SUMMARY

Chapter 8 emphasized the importance of information literacy and its role in learning and professional development in the twenty-first century. You were introduced to a variety of information sources, including those in libraries and on the Internet. You learned the fundamentals of library organization, common reference tools, and using them for research. Online reference tools were also reviewed, with an emphasis on using search engines, databases, and other electronic resources. Concepts and guidelines regarding plagiarism were reviewed and you were reminded to apply them to your research. Finally, you learned how to evaluate the credibility of electronic resources.

The ability to use information wisely is critical to your learning and success in school as well as in the workplace. Concepts of information literacy can also be applied to your personal concerns and development, such as financial planning and developing other areas of personal interest.

POINTS TO KEEP IN MIND

In this chapter, a number of main points were discussed in detail:

- Information literacy means being competent in locating, using, and evaluating information efficiently and effectively.

- Information literacy is essential for school and ultimately workplace success.

- Information-literate individuals are able to locate and use many different resources, including general and subject-specific dictionaries, thesauruses, encyclopedias, almanacs, handbooks, atlases, directories, databases, periodicals, and multimedia materials.

- Libraries are highly organized and use either the Library of Congress Classification or the Dewey Decimal System to physically arrange their materials as well as to identify materials in their cataloging system.

- Information-literate individuals know how to use a library's cataloging system, Library of Congress subject headings, call numbers, indexes, subject directories, and search engines to efficiently search for and find information, either in a physical library or on the Internet.

- Information-literate individuals are aware of and know how to find other sources of information on the Internet such as Web portals, professional and trade organizations, and multimedia.

- Information-literate individuals understand the basic legalities of copyright and appropriate citation methods, as well as other strategies to avoid plagiarism.

- Information-literate individuals understand basic search strategies to answer school and workplace problems.

- Information-literate individuals know how to evaluate the credibility of information they find on the Internet and understand the importance of doing so.

LEARNING OBJECTIVES REVISITED

Review the learning objectives for this chapter and rate your level of achievement for each objective using the rating scale provided. For each objective on which you do not rate yourself as a 3, outline a plan of action that you will take to fully achieve the objective. Include a time frame for this plan.

1 = did not successfully achieve objective

2 = understand what is needed, but need more study or practice

3 = achieved learning objective thoroughly

	1	2	3
Define *information literacy* and explain the necessity for developing these skills for academic and career success.	☐	☐	☐
Describe common library resources and explain their use in finding school- and career-related information.	☐	☐	☐
Demonstrate the ability to use Internet resources effectively in research.	☐	☐	☐
Demonstrate the ability to assess the credibility of information sources.	☐	☐	☐
Define *copyright* and *plagiarism* and demonstrate the ability to avoid plagiarism and cite resources correctly.	☐	☐	☐

Steps to Achieve Unmet Objectives

Steps   Due Date

1. _____   _____

2. _____   _____

3. _____   _____

4. _____   _____

SUGGESTED ITEMS FOR LEARNING PORTFOLIO

▶ Resource List: A list of library resources that will be useful for work and career research.

▶ Journal Analysis: A critique of an article in a refereed journal in your field of study.

▶ Web site Evaluation Checklist: A checklist you can use for assessing any Web site.

REFERENCES

American Library Association. (2004). *Information Literacy Competency Standards for Higher Education.* Retrieved March 3, 2005, from http://www.ala.org/ala/acrl/acrlstandards/informationliteracycompetency.htm

OCLC Online Computer Library Center, Inc. (2003). *Summaries: DDC Dewey Decimal Classification.* Retrieved March 3, 2005, from http://www.oclc.org/dewey/resources/summaries/deweysummaries.pdf

8

CHAPTER OUTLINE

Importance of Communication: An Overview

Effective Verbal Communication

Effective Written Communication

Tools to Assist with Writing

Technology and Written Communication

9 Communication Skills for Student Success

CHAPTER

THE BIG PICTURE

LEARNING OBJECTIVES

By the end of this chapter, you will achieve the following objectives:

▶ Explain the importance of good listening skills.

▶ List reasons why listening can be difficult.

▶ Explain the benefits and characteristics of assertive communication.

▶ Discuss considerations that should be made when sending an e-mail.

▶ Describe how professionalism is demonstrated in written communication.

▶ Explain the purpose of utilizing open-ended questions versus closed questions.

▶ Recognize the importance of body language.

▶ Explain the importance of effective communication.

▶ Demonstrate the ability to create a visual presentation.

▶ Demonstrate the ability to conduct professional correspondence.

TOPIC SCENARIO

After graduation Elizabeth Lanham began searching for a job. In the first two weeks she had sent out 25 resumes. She followed up appropriately, checking to find out when interviews might be taking place and if she was a candidate for consideration. Weeks went by, resumes continued to be sent, but Elizabeth still did not get any interviews. Over time Elizabeth began to wonder why she had not even gotten one call from all the resumes she had sent. She knew she was well qualified for the entry-level jobs she was applying for. After six months Elizabeth finally got her first interview. It wasn't until this first interview that Elizabeth finally found out why she had not been receiving any earlier calls for potential jobs. During the interview Elizabeth was informed that her resume and cover letter had spelling and grammar errors. The interviewee said that Elizabeth was very qualified for the job but that the lack of attention given to her resume and cover letter had indicated a lack of attention to detail that could affect her ability to perform the required job duties. Elizabeth did eventually get a job. By using the interviewee's feedback, Elizabeth made the necessary changes and corrections to her documents so they exhibited the professionalism required for employment. Based on this short description, answer the following questions:

▶ Is it right for employers to rule out applicants due to errors on the resume and/or cover letter? If so, why? If not, why not?

▶ How important do you think written and spoken communication will be in the job that you will be seeking after graduation?

▶ What can Elizabeth do in future written communication to make sure she shows professionalism?

▶ If you lack skills in either written or spoken communications, how do you plan on improving?

▶ What sources might be available to you for improving these skills?

IMPORTANCE OF COMMUNICATION: AN OVERVIEW

As illustrated in Elizabeth's story, it is important to develop excellent communication skills. The significance of effective written and spoken communication skills cannot be understated. In any profession, individuals are valued for their ability to communicate effectively. The focus of this chapter

9

REFLECTION QUESTIONS

- How effective are your communication skills?
- How could you improve your communication?

is to review the skills needed for effective communication in both academic and professional settings. Developing these skills while in school will make a difference to your success as a professional.

EFFECTIVE VERBAL COMMUNICATION

Effective verbal communication is a fundamental skill. Technical aptitude is more useful when it can be expressed clearly. Your success can depend on your ability to apply and communicate your knowledge. Learning how to speak effectively in the classroom and as a professional begins with understanding the basics of effective communication. Communication can be divided into two parts:

▶ The Sender: the individual expressing his or her needs, feelings, thoughts, and opinions

▶ The Receiver: the individual listening and understanding what is being communicated

Effective communication occurs when the receiver of the information interprets and understands the sender's message in the same way the sender intends it.

LISTENING

Listening is one of the most challenging aspects of communication. Ineffective listening can be caused by

▶ preoccupation and lack of attention

▶ thinking rather than listening

▶ closed-minded thinking

▶ prejudging the speaker or judging what is being said

It is important to make the distinction between hearing and listening. Effective listening begins with taking time to understand what the speaker is thinking and feeling from his or her perspective. To listen adequately involves actively participating in the communication process by focusing on what the speaker is saying; attending to spoken elements as well as unspoken elements, such as emotion and body language; and concentrating on the present moment. Active participation cannot be accomplished if you are preoccupied, thinking about other topics, or anticipating what the "right" answer will be to what the speaker is saying.

? CRITICAL THINKING QUESTION

9–1. What is your reaction to the following statement? "Everyone must have excellent spoken and written communication skills to be successful."

© BananaStock Ltd.

Effective communication requires careful and focused attention, clear expression of thoughts and feelings, and mutual respect.

▶ REFLECTION QUESTIONS

• Are you a good listener?
• How might you be able to improve your listening skills?
• What makes listening difficult for you?

9

EFFECTIVE LISTENING

1. Take the time to understand what the speaker is saying.

2. Take the speaker's perspective.

3. Attend to spoken as well as unspoken elements.

? CRITICAL THINKING QUESTIONS

Consider the following scenario and answer the questions that follow.

You are the group leader for a project at your place of employment. One of your team members contributes effectively during group meetings but does not look group members in the eye when speaking. You begin to hear comments and remarks—not all of them kind—about this individual and her lack of eye contact. You suspect that her lack of eye contact may be due to cultural influence.

9–2. How do you approach the group?

9–3. How do you address the issue with the individual?

? CRITICAL THINKING QUESTION

9–4. What other body language examples can you think of? What clues do you think these movements and behaviors reveal?

▶ REFLECTION QUESTION

• Think of a conversation you recently had. Did the individual you were speaking with exhibit any body language? If so, what do you think the body language was telling you?

BODY LANGUAGE

Individuals often communicate feelings or thoughts with their body language.

Arms folded across chest, lack of eye contact, and fidgeting are elements of body language that can be revealing. Arms folded may signal that the individual does not care about what is being said. Lack of eye contact can indicate that the individual feels uncomfortable. Evaluating how others perceive your body language is important. Understanding how others may be interpreting your gestures and movements may help you gain insight into the effectiveness of your communication.

It is important to remember that Western interpretations of body language may differ from interpretations in other cultures. For example, in many Asian cultures, making eye contact can be interpreted as a lack of respect for authority. Avoid jumping to conclusions and consider that if an individual has been raised with certain cultural expectations, these characteristics are deeply ingrained and are to be respected. If certain behavioral nuances interfere with communication, consider cultural diversity. Work collaboratively to achieve an understanding.

Although body language is important to consider during communication, caution should be taken to avoid overinterpretation or misinterpretation. Taking all aspects of communication into consideration is important, so be aware of the other components of communication as well. Use a combination of cues from listening, hearing, and interpreting body language to accurately understand what the receiver is communicating verbally and nonverbally.

INTERPRETING BODY LANGUAGE

1. Be aware of how your body language is being interpreted. You may be conveying an unintended message.

2. Consider that certain gestures and other body language can be interpreted differently by individuals from diverse cultures.

3. Be careful not to overinterpret the meaning of body language.

9

QUESTIONING TECHNIQUES

Asking appropriate questions is another important element of effective communication. Learning how to use questions effectively to discover information is a helpful tool in improving communication. There are two general types of questions: open-ended questions and closed questions.

Open-ended questions require more than a yes or no answer from the receiver. The purpose of asking open-ended questions is to gain more detailed information. An example of an open-ended question would be, "When should open-ended questions be used instead of closed questions?"

Closed questions are typically used to confirm information and often require one or two words to answer. For instance, "Did you go to the office on Monday or Tuesday?" or "Did you say that the test is on Wednesday?"

success steps

USING EFFECTIVE QUESTIONING TECHNIQUES

1. Use open-ended questions to gain detailed information.
2. Use closed questions to confirm information.
3. Use the appropriate type of question to facilitate communication.

ASSERTIVENESS

Assertiveness is the ability to express your beliefs, needs, feelings, and opinions in a manner that clearly makes your point, but that is not intimidating and demonstrates respect for the feelings and opinions of the receiver of your message.

To better understand assertive communication, it is helpful to compare it with other styles that are usually less effective. Consider the following communication styles:

▶ **Aggressive.** Aggressive communication typically conveys anger and impatience and is generally abrasive. Aggressive communication is typically characterized by a raised voice, strong gesturing, glaring eyes, and harsh words. Aggressive communication tends to alienate the receiver of the message and hinders communication.

▶ **Passive.** A passive communication style is characterized by a soft voice, lack of eye contact, and a tendency to avoid stating needs, feelings, and opinions. Passive communication can avoid immediate conflict, but can leave the passive sender feeling "walked on" and as if his or her feelings and wishes are not honored.

? CRITICAL THINKING QUESTIONS

Evaluate the following scenarios and determine what type of question needs to be asked. Indicate the type of question that should be used and then write an appropriate question for each scenario.

9–5. You're at the office and you can't figure out what software the manager wants you to download.
Type: _____
Question: _____

9–6. At your job you need to obtain a patient's history during a physical exam. What might you ask when obtaining a patient's history?
Type: _____
Question: _____

9–7. You are in class and you are really struggling with understanding what is on the board.
Type: _____
Question: _____

9

▶ **Passive-aggressive.** Passive-aggressive communication occurs when feelings of anger or discontent are expressed passively. An example is the individual who, following a meeting with a coworker, smiles and acts as though nothing is wrong. However, he is actually angry and walks out of the office, slamming the door to express his feelings.

▶ **Assertive.** The individual using an assertive communication style expresses his or her opinions and feelings directly using carefully chosen words. Tone of voice is firm, yet calm and nonabrasive, and is modulated at a conversational level. The sender of the assertive message actively listens to the response of the receiver and respectfully acknowledges the sender's position. Eye contact is direct, but not glaring or threatening.

Developing Assertive Communication Skills

There may be situations in which an aggressive or passive communication style is appropriate and effective. However, generally, and especially in the workplace, an assertive communication style is preferred and usually most effective. It is important to remember that using an assertive style does not necessarily get you what you want, but it may maximize your chances or promote a favorable compromise. Consider the following suggestions for communicating assertively:

▶ **Know what you want.** Clearly identify what you want from a specific communication. Doing so will help you express yourself more clearly and support you in knowing where you can compromise.

▶ **Understand your feelings.** Knowing your feelings will help you to express them clearly, which can serve to clarify a situation. For example, saying "I am confused about the messages I am receiving" conveys that you are open to hearing clarification and correcting any misunderstandings. Expressing feelings has the added benefit of humanizing the communication.

▶ **Use "I" statements.** The statement "I am confused about the messages I am receiving" puts the responsibility on the sender of the message. An "I" message avoids blame, which can be implied in messages that begin with "you." Consider the difference between "I am confused about the messages I am receiving" and "You are sending confusing messages." An "I" message indicates that the sender is taking responsibility, while a "you" message tends to sound accusatory and may put the receiver on the defensive, hindering the communication process. Use "I" statements to express your feelings, needs, opinions, and wishes.

9

▶ **Communicate from a "win-win" position.** Be prepared by knowing the points on which you are willing to compromise and be willing to negotiate when appropriate. Use "I" statements to express points on which you are unable or unwilling to compromise.

success steps

COMMUNICATING ASSERTIVELY

1. Clearly identify what you want or need.
2. Understand your feelings and how they relate to what you want.
3. Use "I" statements.
4. Approach the situation with a win-win attitude.

APPRECIATING DIVERSITY

Interacting effectively with others requires an appreciation of each person as an individual. Culture and environment can have a significant impact on communication patterns. Words can have different meanings depending on an individual's culture. Identifying the cultural background of individuals can minimize or avoid confusion or misunderstandings during communication. Home environment can also influence an individual's use of words. Grammar and concepts such as assertiveness can also vary depending on an individual's upbringing. When communicating with others, it is helpful to be considerate and not be too quick to judge an individual's word choice or communication abilities.

VERBAL COMMUNICATION IN THE CLASSROOM

Sending and receiving messages through listening, evaluating body language, and questioning are all parts of the communication process and are critical for successful interaction in the classroom. Learning to communicate effectively in the classroom provides good practice opportunities for developing professional interpersonal skills required for employment. Classroom communication involves both the written and spoken word. It is important to develop your skills in both areas.

There are many opportunities for verbal communication in the classroom, including group activities, discussions, questions, and presentations. To optimize the use of these forums, it is important to follow some simple rules.

▶ **Participate in group activities**. Group activities are successful for individual members and the group only if all members participate. Participation includes not only completing activities but

REFLECTION QUESTIONS

- Is your communication style usually passive, passive-aggressive, aggressive, or assertive? What examples can you give to support your observation?
- What changes might you make to improve your communication style? How would making a change enhance your communications?

REFLECTION QUESTIONS

- In your communication with others, how do you demonstrate appreciation for diversity in your audience?
- How can you increase your sensitivity to diverse communication practices?

Learning to communicate effectively in the classroom provides good practice opportunities for developing the professional interpersonal skills required for employment.

9

communicating clearly with team members as well. To facilitate group communication, it is helpful for group members to establish guidelines and standards for effective communication. Guidelines should also define group etiquette and expectations for respectful and professional communication between group members. Establishing acceptable methods for communication also supports effective communication. For example, the group may choose electronic forms such as e-mail and bulletin boards for communicating with group members and may limit telephone calls to certain hours.

▶ **Ask questions.** Opportunities to ask questions in class offer an excellent chance to confirm your understanding of material and clarify information. Different types of questions can be utilized in the classroom, but always understand your purpose prior to asking. For example, clarifying information may require a closed question, while further explanation of information may be achieved by asking an open-ended question. Although it is said "no question is stupid," do try to utilize class time appropriately. Some questions are best answered in a one-on-one meeting with the instructor rather than during class. Speaking up in class also provides an opportunity to practice making inquiries and speaking up in a group of colleagues, which will be expected in the workplace.

▶ **Develop listening skills.** Listening is an important element of asking and receiving information in class. Listening in class may involve skills other than those used in conversation. For example, in class you may listen for specific information. During the listening process, you may also be actively thinking about how information relates to your existing knowledge and writing notes accordingly. You will balance actively listening to the instructor with recording significant notes for meaningful study at a later time.

▶ **Participate in class discussion.** Instructors sometimes ask reflection questions and critical thinking questions to encourage students to share their opinions and ideas. In-class discussions work best if all students actively participate. Discussion is an excellent way to expand your thinking and understanding of the material and develop critical analysis and thinking skills. Students who develop critical thinking abilities gain a valuable tool that will be appreciated later in their careers. Developing respect for diverse opinions and viewpoints during discussions is also important for successful classroom interaction and is critical to success in the workplace. Demonstrating an appreciation for all opinions, regardless of whether or not you agree, as well as learning to disagree respectfully are basic professional communication skills.

▶ **Give presentations.** In-class presentations require both written and verbal communication skills, both of which improve and become easier with practice. Students need to embrace the opportunities to hone these skills in the classroom. You may find it helpful to practice your presentation in front of the instructor or a small group of peers to gain confidence prior to presenting to the entire class. Other factors in developing presentation skills include allowing enough time to become familiar with the material and revise as needed, maintaining the organization of material during preparation and presentation, and practicing speaking during class discussions. Pay attention to how classmates interact and speak, and learn from observing others. Use opportunities to speak outside of class as practice. When you speak, practice supporting your statements with verifiable facts. If possible, interact with the professional world by working or participating in internship opportunities. Developing confidence and skill at giving presentations will be a valued skill during your career (Gordon, n.d.).

To summarize, effective verbal communication skills are learned. As a student, take advantage of every opportunity to learn and grow in this area. Employers will expect excellent verbal communication skills, and your overall success depends on these skills.

---

success steps

COMMUNICATING EFFECTIVELY IN THE CLASSROOM

1. Actively participate in and contribute to group activities.
2. Ask questions in class.
3. Develop your listening skills.
4. Actively participate in class discussion.
5. Give presentations to develop both oral and written communication skills.

EFFECTIVE WRITTEN COMMUNICATION

Much like oral communication, communicating effectively in writing requires developing skills and taking the time to write correctly. Well-written communication delivers your message with clarity and effectiveness. Poorly written communication can cause confusion and misunderstandings. As with spoken communication, effective written communication is critical to success not only in school but also in the business environment.

9

WRITTEN COMMUNICATION IN THE WORKPLACE

Examples of written communication in the workplace include completing inventory forms, writing financial statements, completing work orders, filling out patient charts, sending electronic messages, and making sales or other types of presentations. Most importantly, daily interactions with colleagues and customers often require clear and effective written communication.

As a student, it is important to clearly understand the requirements that future employers will expect from you as a professional and to practice and apply these skills in the classroom. Written communication is effective when attention is given to the following elements:

> **Professionalism.** Professionalism is indicated by the appearance of the communication. For example, the appearance of a letter can indicate professionalism or a lack of care. Written communication that has grammatical errors or misspellings presents an unprofessional image. In correspondence, elements such as font selection, paper quality, organization, and neatness convey professionalism. Likewise, the manner in which an e-mail is written can either increase your professional credibility or diminish it.

> **Organization.** Organization is critical to professional image. If a term paper is disorganized, the information in the paper may be misunderstood, resulting in a poor grade. A business proposal that is well organized is more likely to achieve a business goal. Effective organization of written communication allows the information to flow, giving the reader a better opportunity to easily comprehend the ideas that are presented.

> **Quality.** Grammatical and punctuation errors, misspellings, smudges, and disorganization of information are examples of a lack of quality in written work. Errors that reflect a lack of quality reflect poorly on your ability to execute other tasks well. While this may seem presumptuous, impressions conveyed by written communication (particularly when your communication is your only introduction to another person) make a strong impact. Developing high standards of quality for written communication while you are in school will lay the foundation for continuing to apply care and attention to details in your future professional communications.

WRITTEN COMMUNICATION IN THE CLASSROOM

The classroom provides an excellent environment for developing your writing skills. Opportunities for developing writing skills in the classroom include note taking, tests, term papers, projects, and presentations. While some of these tasks seem a bit mundane, practicing clarity of written expression in each will contribute to your overall skill development, as well as enhance your learning.

It is important to be clear regarding what the instructor requires. Meet the requirements and go beyond them to cover your topic in a thorough manner that reflects high standards. Keep in mind that the quality of work done for classroom assignments should represent not only what is required in the classroom, but should reflect the type of work you would do on the job. Also, demonstrating writing capabilities in the classroom can be to your benefit if you use the instructor as an employment reference.

Plagiarism

Plagiarism was covered in detail in chapter 5, but any discussion on written communication merits reference to the significance of plagiarism. When completing any written work in the classroom or the workplace, the ethical and legal ramifications of plagiarism are critical. Review chapter 5 and apply methods for avoiding plagiarism to all of your written work.

apply it

Plagiarism Research

GOAL: To develop a better understanding of what plagiarism is and how to avoid it.

STEP 1: Using Internet or library sources, research more about what constitutes plagiarism and how you can avoid it as a student.

STEP 2: Write a short paper regarding your findings. Cite the material used in your research.

Presentations

Various software programs have significantly changed how the written component of classroom presentations is created. Software programs such as Microsoft PowerPoint, Macromedia Director, Corel Presentations, Lotus Freelance Graphics, and Harvard Graphics give individuals the opportunity to produce highly visual presentations. The written component is displayed visually in this type of presentation, making clearly written and precise communication all the more critical. The purpose of using a presentation tool is to enhance the material and visually convey the message. Presentations that have a clear message, are well organized, and are visually appealing will be received more positively.

The following recommendations for creating electronic presentations are based on Hakim (2005):

- Know the purpose of the presentation and who your audience will be.

- Make sure the colors and font styles chosen for your presentation don't cause the audience to focus on the colors and styles versus the content. Colors and styles should be appealing and easy to read, but not the center of attention.

- Have a headline for each slide to focus your audience on each topic presented.

- Use background colors that affect your audience positively. Different colors can create different feelings.

- Make sure your lettering can be clearly seen. For instance, depending upon the background color, your ink may be more visible if it is white instead of black.

- Have your colors complement each other. Colors that do not go well together will be distracting to your audience.

- Use a font that is not too busy. Typically, Arial and Times fonts are chosen for their simple and plain appearance.

- Pay attention to font size. A general rule of thumb is to make sure your audience in the back of the room can read each line clearly. Less than 22-point font will be very difficult to read. Larger than 36 point may be overwhelming.

- As much as possible, limit bulleted items to one or two lines. Bulleted items should be written in phrases rather than full sentences.

- Make sure slides are not overwhelming with either images or text.

- Only use clip art, animations, and other visual aids if they strengthen your message. Remember the "KISS" rule: "Keep It Simple, Silly!"

- Review each slide for accuracy prior to presenting.

- Before the presentation, be familiar with the equipment you will use and have a backup plan, such as handouts, in the event the equipment malfunctions.

- When showing the slide presentation, be sure you are facing the audience.

9

success steps

GIVING EFFECTIVE ELECTRONIC PRESENTATIONS

1. Have a purpose that applies to your audience.

2. Use colors, design, and font styles that are appealing but not the focus of attention.

3. Select a plain font (such as Arial or Verdana) that is of an appropriate size (22–36 point).

4. Limit bullet points to one or two lines.

5. Write bullet points in phrases rather than sentences.

6. Use clip art and images only to illustrate your point. Too much embellishment detracts from the presentation.

7. Review carefully for accuracy before presenting.

8. Face the audience, not the slides.

REFLECTION QUESTIONS

• How much experience have you had in giving presentations?
• What strengths and weaknesses do you think your presentation skills have?
• How do you plan on improving your presentation skills?

apply it

Presentation Tool Analysis

GOAL: To demonstrate the ability to effectively communicate within a team environment, to analyze a presentation tool, and to produce a good presentation.

STEP 1: Form a group of no more than four students.

STEP 2: Each group should research one presentation tool. For instance, Group 1 may research everything about PowerPoint. Group 2 can research what the presentation tool Macromedia Director offers. Group 3 would research Lotus Freelance Graphics.

STEP 3: After each group has conducted its research, students should write a brief analysis of their findings.

STEP 4: Each group should prepare a presentation of its brief analysis. If possible, have each group use the tool it researched as its presentation tool. If only one tool is available in the classroom, all students should use that tool for their presentations.

STEP 5: Consider putting this Presentation Tool Analysis project in your Learning Portfolio.

9

TOOLS TO ASSIST WITH WRITING

In addition to the numerous articles on effective writing that can be found on the Internet, there are a variety of available tools that are worthwhile for use in the classroom and later in business. A few of these tools include:

- dictionary
- thesaurus
- *The Elements of Style* by Strunk and White
- *Modern Language Association Handbook* (MLA style)
- *Publication Manual of the American Psychological Association* (APA style)
- Turabian's *A Manual for Writers of Term Papers, Theses, and Dissertations* (simplified Chicago style)
- software programs such as ScholarWord
- campus resources, such as writing labs, tutors, and your instructor

IMPROVING YOUR WRITING SKILLS

Employers often indicate that writing is one of the most desirable skills a job applicant can possess. Kaplan (2004) offers the following suggestions for improving writing skills:

- Prepare an outline. Use the outline to indicate what needs to be included in the finished piece of writing and to organize its content.
- Write a draft. A draft is just that. At the draft stage, don't worry about spelling, word choice, or grammar. Simply express your thoughts and ideas.
- Correct spelling and review the document for improvement on word choice. Planning ahead and managing your time will leave you ample time to review and revise.
- Use the tools mentioned previously to assist in improving word choice, grammar, and style.
- Write the final draft, paying attention to choice of words and important details such as spelling and grammar. Allow ample time to set the final draft aside for a day or so and review it with a fresh perspective. Make revisions as needed based on your final review. If the content is not of a confidential nature, you might ask a trusted colleague to proofread the document.
- Write as often as possible and consider writing to be a skill that can be worked on and developed. Competence and confidence develop with practice.

9

success steps

COMMUNICATING EFFECTIVELY IN WRITING

Step 1: Budget your time so that you have time to write several drafts as well as review and modify the final copy.

Step 2: Prepare an outline to organize your thoughts.

Step 3: Write a draft to get your thoughts down on paper. Don't worry about spelling, grammar, and neatness at this point—just get the thoughts recorded.

Step 4: Review your draft, correct errors, and modify word choice as needed.

Step 5: Use tools such as those mentioned in this chapter (dictionary, thesaurus, and style guides) to assist in word choice and other aspects of composition.

Step 6: Write the final draft.

Step 7: Set the final draft aside for a day or so and review it with fresh eyes.

Step 8: Ask a trusted colleague to review the final draft if the material is not of a confidential nature.

Step 9: Take advantage of every opportunity to practice writing.

TECHNOLOGY AND WRITTEN COMMUNICATION

Advancements in technology have made effective written communication an even greater requirement. The speed at which electronic communication takes place requires thoughtfulness and attention to tone, choice of words, and accuracy.

E-MAIL

With the increased use of e-mail as a communication tool, knowing how to use e-mail effectively is important. As with any type of written communication, attention should be paid to who the audience is and the purpose of the e-mail. A social e-mail will be different from an e-mail sent for business. Dowling (n.d.) suggests the following tips for writing e-mail:

❯ Prior to sending an e-mail, review it to determine if it is clear, concise, useful, and necessary.

❯ Remember that you can be held accountable for whatever you write.

Using electronic communication, such as e-mail, requires attention to accuracy, detail, and rules of etiquette.

9

▌ Be aware of the length of the e-mail. At times, it might be more effective to write a short note with more detailed information included as an attachment.

▌ E-mail is not always confidential. Send only that which you don't mind having shared. Select other forms of communication, such as a face-to-face meeting or regular mail, for certain types of communication.

▌ As with any correspondence, be professional. E-mail is not to be used for disciplining the reader.

▌ Make sure your e-mail is necessary. If you send too many unnecessary e-mails containing jokes and other trivial communications, receivers of your e-mail may choose to ignore messages from you that may be important. Be aware that in the workplace, sending e-mails of a nonprofessional nature may violate company technology use policy.

▌ Use grammar and punctuation that reflects traditional written communication. Appropriate punctuation makes the message easier to read and reflects on your professionalism.

▌ Observe e-mail etiquette (also called *netiquette*). There are expectations that apply uniquely to e-mail. For example, using all capital letters is considered to be "yelling at" or responding aggressively to your reader. When appropriate, carefully placed capitals can provide emphasis. Using all lowercase does not follow the rules of English grammar and usage.

▌ Use the Subject line appropriately to catch the attention of the receiver. The subject line should accurately (but briefly) describe the content of the e-mail.

▌ Always proofread your e-mail before sending it. Make sure it represents you professionally.

success steps

SENDING PROFESSIONAL E-MAIL

1. Remember that you are accountable for what you write in e-mail.

2. Keep the e-mail brief, with concise information. If a more detailed explanation is needed, consider sending it as an attachment.

3. Send only necessary e-mail. Sending jokes and trivial communications may cause recipients to ignore your e-mail.

4. Know your organization's e-mail policy. There may be consequences for sending e-mail that is not job related.

9

5. Remember that e-mail is not confidential and that records are available.

6. Use traditional grammar and spelling rules.

7. Observe netiquette.

8. Use the subject line to communicate what the e-mail is about.

9. Maintain professionalism. Do not write an e-mail when you are angry or to discipline someone.

10. Proofread your e-mail before sending.

REFLECTION QUESTION

• When writing professional e-mail, how might you change your writing style from that used for social e-mails?

apply it

Style Research

GOAL: To develop a clearer understanding regarding requirements stated in the MLA and APA handbooks.

STEP 1: Research the requirements set forth by the MLA and APA style books (the *Modern Language Association Handbook* and the *Publication Manual of the American Psychological Association*).

STEP 2: Compare and contrast the style suggestions and write a brief explanation of both styles.

STEP 3: Prepare to share your thoughts with the class.

STEP 4: Consider placing this worksheet in your Learning Portfolio.

CHAPTER SUMMARY

This chapter introduced elements of communication that are important to success in school and in the workplace. Listening, nonverbal gestures, questioning, and assertive communication were emphasized as significant elements of oral communication. Professional presentation, quality, and clarity were emphasized as aspects of effective written communication. Considerations specific to electronic communications and presentations were also reviewed.

Effective communication is a skill that is foundational to many other skills and to success in school and the workplace. Your development of all of the skills addressed in *100% Student Success* can be enhanced by effective communication abilities. You are encouraged to consider how developing your communication skills can support all of your academic and professional endeavors.

9

POINTS TO KEEP IN MIND

In this chapter, the following main points were discussed in detail:

▶ Communication has two participating parties: the sender and the receiver.

▶ Lack of attention and closed-minded thinking can reduce the effectiveness of listening.

▶ By listening, hearing, and interpreting body language, the receiver may more accurately understand what the sender is communicating verbally and nonverbally.

▶ Two general types of questions are open ended and closed.

▶ Respect for individual diversity is essential for effective communication.

▶ Learning how to communicate effectively in the classroom offers good practice for the professional communication skills required for employment.

▶ In-class group activities are successful only if all team members participate.

▶ Listening well facilitates learning from in-class questions.

▶ Giving attention to professionalism, organization, and quality of the material makes written communication more effective.

▶ Plagiarism is using another person's ideas or words without giving the author appropriate credit.

▶ The purpose of using presentation tools is to enhance the material and visually convey the message.

LEARNING OBJECTIVES REVISITED

Review the learning objectives for this chapter and rate your level of achievement for each objective using the rating scale provided. For each objective on which you do not rate yourself as a 3, outline a plan of action that you will take to fully achieve the objective. Include a time frame for this plan.

1 = did not successfully achieve objective

2 = understand what is needed, but need more study or practice

3 = achieved learning objective thoroughly

	1	2	3
Explain the importance of good listening.	☐	☐	☐
List reasons for why listening can be difficult.	☐	☐	☐
Explain ways to avoid plagiarism.	☐	☐	☐
Discuss considerations that should be made when sending an e-mail.	☐	☐	☐

9

	1	2	3
Describe how professionalism is demonstrated in written communication.	☐	☐	☐
Explain the purpose of utilizing open-ended questions versus closed questions.	☐	☐	☐
Recognize the importance of body language.	☐	☐	☐
Explain the importance of effective verbal communication.	☐	☐	☐
Demonstrate the ability to create a visual presentation.	☐	☐	☐
Demonstrate the ability to conduct professional correspondence.	☐	☐	☐

Steps to Achieve Unmet Objectives

Steps   Due Date

1. _____   _____

2. _____   _____

3. _____   _____

4. _____   _____

SUGGESTED ITEMS FOR LEARNING PORTFOLIO

▶ Reflection and Critical Thinking Questions: Include your written responses to these questions. Use them to review your development over time.

▶ Presentation Tool Analysis

▶ Style Research

REFERENCES

Dowling, E. (n.d.). 10 tips for effective e-mail. Mind Tools. Retrieved February 10, 2005, from http://www.mindtools.com/email.html

Gordon, D. E. (n.d.). Five keys to acquiring better verbal communication skills. CollegeRecruiter.com. Retrieved February 10, 2005, from http://www.collegerecruiter.com/pages/articles/article146.htm

Hakim, C. (2005). Essentials of effective PowerPoint presentations— PowerPoint presentations that work. Retrieved May 24, 2006, from http://www.unleash.com/chakim/essentials/index.asp

Kaplan, R. M. (2004). You can improve your written communication skills. Retrieved February 20, 2005, from http://www.job-resources.com/0103tip.htm

9

© Digital Vision

CHAPTER OUTLINE

The Importance of Understanding Human Behavior: An Overview

Influences on Human Behavior

Self-Image and Self-Esteem: An Overview

Effects of Success and Failure

Motivation

10 Human Behavior

THE BIG PICTURE

LEARNING OBJECTIVES

By the end of this chapter, you will achieve the following objectives:

▶ Explain the importance of understanding human behavior in school and the workplace.

▶ Describe three major influences on human behavior and the possible effects of each.

▶ Compare self-concept and self-esteem.

▶ Describe how self-image influences behavior.

▶ Describe steps for developing a realistic self-image.

▶ Describe steps for developing a healthy self-esteem.

▶ Illustrate the relationship of self-esteem to successful and unsuccessful performance.

▶ Describe needs and motivation according to Maslow and McClelland.

▶ Describe the relationship of motivation to success and failure.

TOPIC SCENARIO

Tim Johnson has been attending the local college for one semester. Tim is an A student. He never has had to struggle with grades, and he is pleased that this trend has continued with his college studies. However, Tim is unhappy. He likes his program, but Tim has the following complaints:

1. Tim feels that his classmates are rude. They never invite him to any social events and they poke fun at him.

2. Tim believes that his instructors pay more attention to other students than to him.

3. Tim believes the paperwork that the financial aid office gave him to fill out is a waste of time and that all the financial aid personnel care about is money.

4. Although career services helped him find a part-time job, Tim doesn't like the job and feels career services could have found him something better.

Based on this short description of Tim's college experience, answer the following questions:

▶ How might Tim's own behavior and attitude be contributing to any of these situations?

▶ Could Tim's view of himself be affecting his view of these situations? If so, how?

▶ Could fear of success be affecting how Tim is evaluating the situations? If so, how?

▶ Instead of just quitting the program, what are some constructive ways Tim can address these issues?

▶ Did you learn anything about yourself through evaluating Tim's situation? If so, what?

THE IMPORTANCE OF UNDERSTANDING HUMAN BEHAVIOR: AN OVERVIEW

Academic success involves more than simply achieving good grades. Success in any environment comes from the ability to interact effectively with others by understanding your own behavior and the behavior of others. Both the academic and work environments can present challenging situations. The ability to establish and maintain effective relationships in and outside of school is an important trait to develop and a desired skill for

Success in school and the professional world requires the ability to interact effectively with others in a variety of settings and situations.

© Digital Vision

10

employment. Successfully working with others requires an understanding of the basic concepts of human behavior.

INFLUENCES ON HUMAN BEHAVIOR

To understand why individuals think or feel certain ways requires exploring what makes people tick. Milliken (1998) suggests the following three factors that influence people's behavior:

▶ **Heredity.** Heredity is what makes individuals unique. Genes determine an individual's physical appearance. Genes can also influence a person's likes, dislikes, abilities, and personality.

▶ **The developmental process.** Humans develop in physical, emotional, intellectual, and spiritual areas. A person's physical health can be greatly influenced by heredity, the environment in which he or she grows up, and the health of his or her mother during pregnancy. Development in each dimension can be affected by environmental and life conditions. For example, individuals from an abusive home situation may show signs of emotional immaturity. For others, spiritual growth may mature more slowly due to upbringing. Ideally, all of these areas are developed and matured.

▶ **Environment.** Environment can be divided into the physical and social environments. The physical environment includes location, climate, level of urbanization, type of living structure, and other tangible resources. Observe that the talents and experiences of an individual who has grown up on a tropical island will be quite different from those of the person from a large northern city. The social environment refers to relationships and the types of human influences that have an impact on an individual as he or she matures. The social environment also has a significant impact on a person. The amount and quality of involvement that an individual has had with people will determine his or her abilities in communication, trust, and nurturing.

Although childhood greatly influences who we are as adults, it is important to understand that as adults we can choose to learn and grow. Recognizing childhood influences on behavior will help in this growth process. "Whereas a child is the helpless victim of developmental influences, an adult can become self-directing. The adult can recognize an undesirable behavior pattern and choose to change it" (Milliken, 1998, p. 51). Reflecting on individual traits, taking responsibility for actions, and improving behavior are some of the primary responsibilities of adults.

It is also important to recognize different abilities and rates of change and to develop patience and understanding for those who may be slower in

REFLECTION QUESTIONS

- What are your beliefs about human behavior?
- How does behavior influence interpersonal relationships?
- How well do you interact with others?
- How might you be able to improve your relationships with others?

? CRITICAL THINKING QUESTION

10–1. What is your reaction to the following statement? "I just want to go to class, do my homework, and get a good job. If I get along with my classmates that's fine; if I don't, that is fine too."

REFLECTION QUESTIONS

- How has your childhood affected who you are as an adult?
- In what areas do you need to develop your skills?
- How will understanding individual differences help you to communicate effectively?

10

apply it

Web Research

GOAL: To learn more about influences on human behavior.

STEP 1: Conduct a Web search for articles on what influences human behavior.

STEP 2: Find one Web site that you consider to be of high credibility and that contains an article that is useful in furthering your knowledge of influences on human behavior.

STEP 3: Read the article and write a brief analysis of your findings. Consider questions such as:

   a. Do you agree with what is being presented? If so, why? If not, why?

   b. What made you think this information had high credibility?

   c. What did you learn about influences on your own behavior?

STEP 4: Consider placing this analysis in your Learning Portfolio.

the growth process. For example, some individuals may be challenged by growing socially, while others may find intellectual growth more demanding. Recognizing these individual differences will help you communicate more effectively with a greater number of people.

PERSONALITY DEVELOPMENT

Another factor that influences human behavior is personality. Table 10–1 presents two theories of how personalities develop.

Eric Erickson was a psychologist who presented a theory that personality is developed throughout the different stages of life, namely, infancy,

TABLE 10–1.   SELECTED THEORIES OF PERSONALITY DEVELOPMENT

Theorists	Ideas on personality development
Erik Erikson	1. Develops over the life span
	2. Affected by the environment
	3. Divided into stages
	4. Each stage has a specific task to be accomplished
	5. Goal is task accomplishment
Abraham Maslow	1. Develops over the life span
	2. Affected by the environment
	3. Divided into needs, which are used as motivators
	4. Goal is self-actualization

Turner, J.S. & Helms, D.B. (1995). Lifespan development (5th ed.). Philadelphia: Harcourt Brace College Publishers.

10

toddlerhood, middle childhood, adolescence, young adulthood, middle adulthood, and late adulthood. Erickson emphasizes that each stage of development presented a major developmental task an individual must accomplish in order to mature optimally.

Abraham Maslow proposed a hierarchy of needs ranging from the most basic survival needs (such as food) to self-actualization needs (such as recognizing and fulfilling one's potential). According to the hierarchy, shown in Figure 10–1, all humans have needs that are satisfied by elements in the environment. Maslow's hierarchy is represented by a triangle. The base of the triangle represents the most basic human survival needs. Each level of the triangle represents an additional need that is met only when the need below it is satisfied. For example, think of the homeless person for whom survival is the primary concern. The homeless person is probably not concerned with self-actualization or other needs higher on Maslow's hierarchy. Another example might be the individual who is facing an abusive situation and is more concerned with safety than love and affection. Needs change as life events occur, and individuals may find themselves at different points in the hierarchy at different times. In addition, needs play a significant role in motivation, which will be discussed later in this chapter.

To summarize, understanding basic theories of human behavior offers individuals the opportunity to appreciate the reasons for people's behaviors. Understanding and consciously considering these influences can provide greater understanding and patience during interactions with others.

Maslow's hierarchy of needs

FIGURE 10–1.

Turner, J.S. & Helms, D.B. (1995). Lifespan development (5th ed.). Philadelphia: Harcourt Brace College Publishers.

---

success steps

CONSIDERATIONS IN UNDERSTANDING HUMAN BEHAVIOR

1. Take a person's heredity and environment into account.
2. Consider the developmental process.
3. Think about childhood influences.
4. Recognize individual differences, strengths, and weaknesses.
5. Consider personality factors.

▶ REFLECTION QUESTIONS

- What level are you at in Maslow's hierarchy of needs?
- What goals might you set that would help fulfill the current needs you have?
- Consider an interaction that you had recently. How can you better understand that interaction based on Maslow's theory?

SELF-IMAGE AND SELF-ESTEEM: AN OVERVIEW

As a student and professional, it is important to recognize how your social needs are being met. The fulfillment of social needs requires having satisfying relationships with others. As pointed out previously, this may be quite

10

difficult for some individuals due to their life experiences. However, recall that adults can make the choice to change and grow. Successful individuals have learned how to have satisfying social interactions. Since a person's self-image and self-esteem can have a great impact on his or her ability to establish and maintain satisfying relationships, understanding these concepts is important.

SELF-IMAGE

Self-image is the way in which we view ourselves, including our abilities, talents, physical appearance, and personality traits. Your self-image can be realistic in terms of your actual attributes, meaning you have a realistic sense of your strengths and weaknesses. Self-image can also be inflated, in which you see your attributes as better than they really are. Conversely, self-image can be low, resulting in a poor evaluation of your own abilities and traits.

Self-image develops over time. What is told to us as children influences what we believe and think about ourselves and others as adults. If a child is told that he or she is fatter than everyone else, then that individual is likely to grow up with the self-image of being fat. A child who brings home a grade of B and is told it isn't as good as an A develops the impression that he or she is successful only if high levels of achievement are attained. Personality traits can be developed in the same manner. For example, if a child is outgoing and this personality trait is encouraged, as an adult his or her outgoing personality will be part of his or her self-image.

The manner in which adults interact with children has a significant impact on their self-image.

Influences of Self-Image

How you see yourself influences many (if not all) aspects of your life. Consider the following examples of areas that can be influenced by your self-image:

▶ **Performance.** The way in which you perceive your abilities influences the way you set goals and ultimately determines your success. For example, an individual with a poor self-image is likely to set lower goals based on how he views his abilities, thus compromising the potential to move ahead. An individual with an inflated self-image may set goals that are too lofty, resulting in failure and a lack of achievement. An objective assessment of skills and abilities leads to an accurate self-image that allows realistic performance and improvement goals to be set.

▶ **Relationships with others.** Your self-image can vary considerably from the picture that others have of you. Your life experiences have developed your perceptions of yourself in a unique way and cause

▶ REFLECTION QUESTIONS

- What is your self-image? How do you perceive yourself?
- What about your self-image do you want to change?

10

you to view yourself differently than others do. Expectations of relationships can vary depending on the way in which the individuals involved perceive themselves and each other. For example, if your supervisor perceives you as less capable than you see yourself, you may feel bored or unchallenged due to his or her low expectations.

▶ **General adjustment.** If self-image issues are having a negative influence on your performance, relationships, or other areas of your life, your general level of adjustment and satisfaction can be affected. If these issues are significant to you, evaluating and understanding the role that your self-image may be playing may be helpful to you.

Creating a Realistically Positive Self-Image

Having a realistic self-image means that you know your strengths and weaknesses. You credit yourself for your skills and talents and set goals to develop areas needing improvement. An important concept to remember is that everyone has strengths as well as weaknesses and that perfection is not the goal. The following suggestions are based on recommendations from Mountain State Centers for Independent Living and are intended to recognize strong attributes as well as put weaknesses in perspective.

▶ **Assess skills realistically.** As discussed previously, our influences from the past can tell us a variety of things, and not all of them are positive. For example, if you have been told you are not good at math, you might believe that and shy away from math courses. In this case, a current assessment of math aptitude would give a more objective assessment than perceptions based on the past. Assess your skills and abilities and realistically determine an objective way to measure them against an accepted standard. Give yourself credit for your strengths and set goals for improvement in areas you wish to develop.

▶ **Avoid exaggeration and the need for perfection.** Many people tend to be highly critical of themselves, resulting in a tendency to exaggerate the negative. For example, if you need to improve certain areas of math performance, it doesn't mean that you can't do any math at all or that you are a failure in school. Conversely, an individual who believes he or she excels in all areas has an equally exaggerated self-image and is set for failure and alienating others. Believing that there is a need to be perfect is another form of exaggeration. There is no need to be able to perform a task perfectly before you can attempt it. Focus on strengths and tasks done well and accept the areas in which improvement is needed.

? **CRITICAL THINKING QUESTIONS**

10–2. What other aspects of life might be influenced by self-image issues?

10–3. How can you evaluate your self-image?

10–4. What are some ways to compare your self-perception with the perceptions that others have of you?

10

▶ **Pay attention to your thoughts.** Monitor your thoughts. If you find yourself exaggerating about your strengths or weaknesses, stop yourself and think about your objective standards. If you do find yourself being excessively negative, set a positive goal and give yourself encouragement on your positive attributes and abilities. Avoid telling yourself that you "should have" or "would have." Don't make unrealistic demands on yourself.

▶ **Focus on the positive.** If you have a tendency to dwell on negative aspects of yourself, take opportunities to consciously focus on positive attributes. Note positive feedback that you get from others, accomplishments that you have made, and jobs done well. Identify the positive characteristics that led to your success.

▶ **Accept responsibility appropriately.** You are in control of your choices and feelings. Assess and understand what is in your control and what is not. Use your skills and attributes to control what you can and avoid frustration by understanding that you are not accountable for or able to fix situations over which you have no control or responsibility.

▶ **Move on from the past.** Examine your perceptions and their origins and decide if they are relevant to where you are today. The messages that come from the past are often simply not true. Use your objective self-assessment to support you in this task.

▶ **Get feedback.** Ask trusted colleagues and associates for feedback. You are the final judge regarding whether or not to accept feedback, but learning how others perceive you will let you know how your perceptions match those of others.

? CRITICAL THINKING QUESTIONS

10–5. What is the relationship of an individual's self-image to his or her overall school performance and academic achievements?

10–6. How might self-image positively affect school performance? How might it affect performance negatively?

success steps

CREATING A POSITIVE SELF-IMAGE

1. Assess your skills objectively and realistically.
2. Avoid exaggeration and the need for perfection.
3. Pay attention to your thoughts. Monitor how you think about yourself.
4. Focus on the positive.
5. Accept responsibility appropriately.
6. Move on from the past. If perceptions are wrong, let them go.
7. Get feedback. Ask how others perceive you.

10

SELF-ESTEEM

Self-esteem is defined as the way an individual feels about him or herself. Self-esteem is closely related to self-image, as an individual may like or dislike what he sees in himself. Similarly, the way in which self-image influences performance and relationships can also influence self-esteem. A poor or unrealistic self-image that negatively affects performance and relationships often results in poor self-esteem. A negative cycle is set when low self-esteem causes an individual to doubt his or her abilities, reinforcing a poor self-image.

The University of Texas at Austin Counseling and Mental Health Center (1999) indicates that positive self-esteem develops when children are praised, receive attention, are respected and listened to, and experience success. Alternatively, low self-esteem is often the result of criticism, harsh discipline, ridicule, a lack of appropriate attention, unrealistic expectations, and experiencing failure. Individuals with positive self-esteem like what they see in their self-image; those with low self-esteem see themselves less positively and tend to be overly critical of their endeavors.

The Influences of Self-Esteem

Consider how you function on a day when you are feeling badly about yourself. Hopefully, this is a temporary state, but the effects of feeling this way can lower your confidence levels, reduce your energy and ability to take on and complete various tasks, negatively influence how you respond to others, and increase anxiety levels. Low self-esteem, which is more continuous than temporary, has the same effects.

Developing Healthy Self-Esteem

As it is possible to develop a positive self-image, it is also possible to build healthy self-esteem. Some of the methods for developing self-esteem reflect the techniques that were discussed for a positive self-image. Having a realistic self-image can contribute to healthy self-esteem by allowing you to recognize your strengths as well as improve areas of weakness or accept them. The following suggestions are based on recommendations from The University of Texas at Austin Counseling and Mental Health Center (1999):

▷ **Use your realistic self-image as a guide.** Develop your self-image. Focus on recognizing both your strengths and weaknesses. Give yourself credit for your achievements and skills and set goals for what you wish to change. Decide what you are willing to accept.

▶ REFLECTION QUESTION

- How do you think your childhood affected your self-esteem?

? CRITICAL THINKING QUESTION

10–7. What events during childhood can you think of that could affect an individual's self-esteem?

10

▶ **Listen to your thoughts.** Pay attention to how you are thinking about yourself, others, and your environment. The messages that you are sending yourself may be based on old experiences or unsubstantiated information and may be detrimental to your self-esteem.

▶ **Use your objective assessment.** Refer back to your objective assessment of your skills, strengths, and weaknesses. Remind yourself of your strong points and the goals toward which you are working. Remember that perfection is unnecessary and impossible.

▶ **Take care of the basics.** Chapter 6 discussed the importance of basic self-management techniques, including healthy nutrition and sleep habits, exercise, organization, and time and financial management. When you attend to your basic needs, you will feel better physically and mentally and have energy available to develop skills and attributes that contribute to healthy self-esteem.

▶ **Use your resources.** As was suggested in the discussion on building a realistic self-image, seek feedback from trusted colleagues. Use the resources available to you through your campus, such as advisors, instructors, and student support services. Trusted resources can assist you in making your objective self-assessment, setting goals, and using your strengths to achieve success.

Accepting constructive criticism from trusted professional colleagues as well as listening to your "inner voice" can be useful in personal relationships.

success steps

DEVELOPING HEALTHY SELF-ESTEEM

1. Use your realistic self-image as a guide.
2. Listen to your thoughts. (How do you think about yourself?)
3. Use your objective assessment.
4. Take care of the basics.
5. Use your resources.

EFFECTS OF SUCCESS AND FAILURE

Self-image and self-esteem are closely related to success and failure. In addition, the effects of your successes and failures can have a great impact on your performance and the development of your abilities. An individual who has experienced repeated failures may be more likely to develop low self-confidence and self-esteem. Figure 10–2 illustrates the cyclic nature of self-image, self-esteem, and performance. When you have a realistic

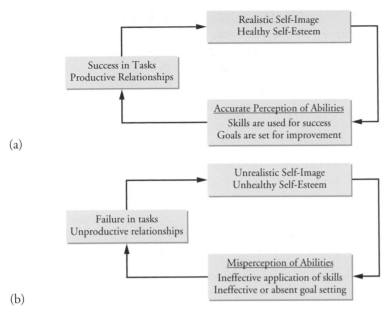

(a)

(b)

FIGURE 10–2. Cycles of self esteem and performance (a): A realistic self image and healthy self esteem have a positive influence on the use of skills and goal setting, resulting in success in tasks and relationships. (b): An unrealistic self image and unhealthy self esteem negatively influence skill use and goal setting, resulting in failure in tasks and relationships.

perception of your strengths and weaknesses, you select tasks to perform that use your strengths and provide an appropriate challenge to develop weaker areas. If you see yourself as capable of something that is actually beyond your abilities, the discrepancy between self-image and actual aptitude can result in disappointing performance and difficulties with colleagues.

Individuals who have high self-esteem have typically experienced more successes than failures and are able to perpetuate successes. From their experiences, they have learned that mistakes and disappointments do happen, but their self-worth is not affected. These individuals are usually able to view failure as a learning experience. Individuals with a less healthy self-image and self-esteem more frequently experience failure at tasks, adding to an unrealistic self-image and unhealthy self-esteem.

Individuals who have multiple failures can develop what is called *failure expectation*. The cycle of failure affects expectations and can be damaging to an individual by creating self-doubt that minimizes chances for future success. Figure 10–3 illustrates failure expectation.

In a similar fashion, success influences how an individual thinks about himself or herself. Recognize that both small and large successes contribute to building self-confidence, which can greatly impact future successes. It is important to recognize *all* successes, such as making a relevant contribution to a class discussion.

? CRITICAL THINKING QUESTION

10–8. Consider the statement, "the discrepancy between self-image and actual aptitude can result in disappointing performance and difficulties with colleagues." Give examples of how this can occur.

10

REFLECTION QUESTIONS

To successfully analyze your task performance, ask yourself the following questions:

- Did I obtain and prepare materials effectively?
- Did I organize my materials effectively?
- Did I manage my time to effectively complete and review the project?
- Did I follow instructions or protocol?
- If I altered instructions or protocol, did I do so for the benefit of my outcomes? Did my changes to instructions or protocol support professional standards and ethics? Did my outcomes improve?
- Did I sequence steps appropriately and effectively?
- Did I pay appropriate attention to details? Were enough details provided to support my project without overwhelming my audience or getting off track?
- Did I work cooperatively with others involved in the task by keeping the good of the group in mind?
- Did I collaborate with others to make the best use of all individual skills in the group?
- Did I review and revise my work? If not, why? If so, what changes were made to this project? What can be applied to future projects?

FIGURE 10–3. The Failure Expectation Cycle illustrates how self doubt and expectations contribute to failure.

The Failure Expectation Cycle, from pg. 81 of Understanding Human Behavior by Mary Elizabeth Milliken, 6th Edition, 1998, Thomson Learning.

Successes are specific to each individual. Avoid comparing yourself to others. For example, for some students, achieving a C in certain subjects is as much of a success as it would be for others to achieve an A. The success might be improving a grade or mastering a difficult concept. If a higher grade can be achieved or is desirable, the objective self-assessment can be used to analyze how improvement can be made for future classes.

Analysis of a particular task can create a learning experience and lay the foundation for future improvement. Task components such as preparing, organizing, managing time, following instructions or protocol, sequencing steps, attending to detail, working cooperatively and collaboratively, and reviewing and revising your work are some of the elements that can be evaluated to support your success and improvement.

apply it

Research and Presentation

GOAL: To help develop an understanding of how culture and environment can affect self-image and self-esteem.

STEP 1: Form groups of no more than four or five students.

STEP 2: Each group should select a culture to research, such as Latin American, Asian, or European.

STEP 3: Each group is to conduct research on the effects that an individual's culture can have on self-image and self-esteem. Consider the elements discussed in the previous sections.

STEP 4: Use a variety of methods of research, such as interviews with individuals from those cultures, books, and articles.

STEP 5: Each group writes a brief report and presents its findings to the class. Visual aids such as PowerPoint, posters, handouts, or overhead transparencies should be used.

STEP 6: Consider putting this Research and Presentation activity in your Learning Portfolio.

Working diligently on school projects and assignments and assessing the reasons for your successes and failures will add to your long-term success.

MOTIVATION

There are various theories about what motivates people. According to Maslow's theory of need, individuals are motivated by the need they are trying to satisfy. For instance, an individual who is driven by the need to survive will be more motivated to do what is necessary to meet that need. The same can be said for an individual who needs to feel loved. Actions that fulfill a certain need will be taken.

David McClelland defined his theory of motivation in terms of various factors that motivate people (Kolb, Osland, & Rubin, 1995). He suggests that three needs motivate individuals: the need for affiliation, the need for power, and the need for achievement. These terms are defined as follows:

▶ **Affiliation.** The individual who is motivated by affiliation seeks strong relationships. As the name suggests, an individuals who is motivated by affiliation needs seeks to be a member of and accepted by a group.

▶ **Power.** Individuals who are motivated by power generally have a need to be in control and to influence others. Being motivated by the need for power can be expressed as positive leadership or negatively, as in cases of manipulation or abuse.

▶ **Achievement.** Individuals with a need for achievement find their motivation in accomplishing their goals and engaging in self-improvement strategies. These individuals tend to take responsibility for their actions and thrive on appropriately difficult challenges. Individuals who are motivated by achievement needs value feedback on their performance and apply it.

10

REFLECTION QUESTIONS

- What motivates you?
- How have your parents or culture influenced your motives for accomplishing certain goals in your life?
- How do your needs affect your motivation at school and work?

McClelland concluded that each individual is motivated by varying degrees of each of these factors. The strength of each motivating need varies depending upon the person. For example, you might be motivated by a high need for achievement, a moderate need for affiliation, and a low need for power. A classmate might be highly motivated by power, moderately motivated by achievement, and minimally motivated by affiliation needs. Culture can affect an individual's motivation. For instance, since power and control are dominant cultural themes in Latin America, an individual from this culture may be motivated by the need for power. Parental influence may also affect how an individual is motivated.

MOTIVATION, SUCCESS, AND FAILURE

An examination of the motivation to achieve reveals a relationship to self-image and self-esteem.

- **Motivation requires an appropriate level of challenge.** Recall that having a realistic self-image allows you to identify strengths and weaknesses and set goals accordingly. Knowing your attributes allows you to be successful, leading to healthy self-esteem. Too much challenge can be intimidating, while too little challenge can result in boredom. Both extremes can decrease motivation. An accurate self-image and healthy self-esteem contribute to motivation by guiding you in the selection of appropriately challenging tasks and goals.

- **People are more motivated when they believe they can affect outcomes.** McClelland's research suggested that individuals are more motivated when they believe that their efforts will influence a result or outcome (Accel-Team.com, n.d.). If your level of challenge is appropriate, you are more likely to believe this to be true.

- **Motivation and achievement are related to personal accomplishment.** Another of McClelland's findings indicated that achievers are more concerned with their personal accomplishment than with external rewards. Recognizing both your large and small successes and setting and meeting achievable goals contribute to your feelings of personal accomplishment.

- **Motivation and achievement are enhanced by feedback and reflection.** Part of motivation is understanding your performance and how to improve it. By thinking about (reflecting on) your performance and getting feedback from trusted individuals, you can increase your motivation levels, as well as develop your self-image and self-esteem.

10

success steps

PRACTICES FOR ENHANCING MOTIVATION

1. Set goals that are appropriately challenging yet achievable.
2. Set goals that allow you to influence the outcome.
3. Focus on your personal accomplishments rather than on external rewards.
4. Reflect on your goals and performance.
5. Obtain feedback from trusted sources.

As a student it is important to understand the motivating factors that led you not only to attend college, but also to succeed. People are motivated internally, so identifying motivating factors and tasks is critical to success. An instructor can tell a student to work hard or study more, but the student must be motivated to do so based on his or her own needs. The instructor's encouragement may support the student's internal motivation, but it is the student's personal incentive that will lead to success.

REFLECTION QUESTIONS

- What is motivating you to attend and complete college?
- What problems can you think of that might deter you from your goal?
- How might you be able to motivate yourself during problem times?

CHAPTER SUMMARY

This chapter focused on elements of human behavior that contribute to success in school and the workplace. The chapter began by emphasizing the importance of understanding behavior in terms of working effectively with other people. A summary of the influences on human behavior, such as heredity, the developmental process, and environment, was provided. Following this general overview, factors that influence individual behavior and success in school were reviewed. Self-image, self-esteem, success and failure, and motivation were discussed in detail.

It is important to consider how other topics in the *100% Student Success* textbook support your behavior and success. For example, goal setting was discussed in Chapter 1. How can you relate goal setting to developing your self-image? How does goal setting relate to motivation? Understanding these types of relationships between concepts presented in the text will help you to make the best use of the information.

10

POINTS TO KEEP IN MIND

In this chapter, numerous main points were discussed in detail:

- Three factors that influence people's behavior are heredity, developmental process, and environment.
- Adults can change their behavior if they so choose.
- Abraham Maslow's hierarchy of needs emphasizes that all humans have basic needs and these needs are affected by the presence or absence of things such as nurturing, acceptance, love, and a sense of belonging and self-worth.
- A person's self-esteem, self-worth, and self-concept can greatly affect his or her ability to have satisfying relationships.
- Self-image is defined as how an individual sees him- or herself.
- Self-esteem is defined as how an individual feels about him- or herself.
- Poor self-esteem affects one's confidence, which can also have a negative impact on the ability to communicate well and effectively interact with others.
- Examples of steps to increase one's self-esteem are practicing self-nurturing and asking for help from others.
- Individuals with multiple failures can develop failure expectation.
- Self-doubt can create such havoc that future success on other tasks can be affected.
- Success comes in many forms, including accomplishing tasks and demonstrating kindness and courtesy.
- Learning from failures is important for future successes.
- People are motivated internally by a combination of the need for affiliation, the need for power, and the need for achievement.
- Setting well-stated and clear goals helps individuals remain motivated.

LEARNING OBJECTIVES REVISITED

Review the learning objectives for this chapter and rate your level of achievement for each objective using the rating scale provided. For each objective on which you do not rate yourself as a 3, outline a plan of action that you will take to fully achieve the objective. Include a time frame for this plan.

1 = did not successfully achieve objective

2 = understand what is needed, but need more study or practice

3 = achieved learning objective thoroughly

	1	2	3
Explain the importance of understanding human behavior in school and in the workplace.	☐	☐	☐
Describe three major influences on human behavior and the possible effects of each.	☐	☐	☐
Describe three major effects of each.	☐	☐	☐
Describe how self-image influences behavior.	☐	☐	☐
Describe steps for developing a realistic self-image.	☐	☐	☐
Describe steps for developing a healthy self-esteem.	☐	☐	☐
Illustrate the relationship of self-esteem to successful and unsuccessful performance.	☐	☐	☐
Describe needs and motivation according to Maslow and McClelland.	☐	☐	☐
Describe the relationship of motivation to success and failure.	☐	☐	☐

Steps to Achieve Unmet Objectives

Steps   Due Date

1. _____   _____

2. _____   _____

3. _____   _____

4. _____   _____

SUGGESTED ITEMS FOR LEARNING PORTFOLIO

▶ Research and Presentation

▶ Web Research

REFERENCES

Accel-Team.com. (n.d.). Employee motivation, the organizational environment, and productivity. David McClelland: Achievement motivation. Retrieved October 13, 2005, from http://www.accel-team.com/human_relations/hrels_06_mcclelland.html

10

Kolb, D. A., Osland, J. S., & Rubin, I. M. (1995). Organizational behavior: An experiential approach (6th ed.). Englewood Cliffs, NJ: Prentice Hall.

Milliken, M. E. (1998). *Understanding Human Behavior* (6th ed.). Clifton Park, NY: Thomson Delmar Learning.

Mountain State Centers for Independent Living. (n.d.). Positive self image and self esteem. Retrieved October 12, 2005, from http://www.mtstcil.org/skills/image-3.html

University of Texas–Austin, Counseling and Mental Health Center. (1999). Better self-esteem. Retrieved March 1, 2005, from http://www.utexas.edu/student/cmhc/booklets/selfesteem/selfest.html

10

Conclusion

MOVING ON FROM HERE

You are now familiar with the many elements that contribute to your success as a student and that provide the foundation for your future success as a professional. You should come away from the *100% Student Success* experience with ideas and strategies for self-management, insight into your learning, and methods for achieving your educational goals.

For now, practice what you have learned. Remember to keep these concepts and ideas foremost in your mind, so that you can readily apply them to your daily activities. Practice will allow techniques and methods to become second nature to you. As you move closer to graduating, and seeking employment, remember that the skills you practice now will contribute to your success in the job search and in the field. When you reach that point, the next books in the *100% Success* series, *100% Job Search Success* and *100% Career Success,* will support you in the continued development of your professional skills.

You have received an effective introduction to the topics presented in *100% Student Success.* You are encouraged to expand your knowledge and pursue areas of interest and to further develop your skills. Use the references provided for each chapter, and pursue additional resources according to your interests and needs.

Again, congratulations on your successes to date, and all the best to you as you pursue your goals.

Index